Modern World Development

For Annabel
Julia
Andrew

Modern World Development

A geographical perspective

Michael Chisholm

BARNES & NOBLE BOOKS
Totowa, New Jersey

First published in the USA 1982 by
BARNES & NOBLE BOOKS
81 Adams Drive
Totowa, New Jersey, 07512

ISBN: 0-389-20320-3 (cloth)
     0-389-20321-1 (paper)

Library of Congress Cataloging in Publication Data

Chisholm, Michael, 1931–
   Modern world development.

   1. Economic development.   2. Geography, Economic.
3. Natural resources.   4. Human capital.   I. Title.
HD75.C48 1982   338.9   82-11404

Contents

108962

Figures

Tables

Preface

The immediate and tangible spur to think and read about the subject-matter of this book was provided by the honour of being elected Junior Vice-President of the Institute of British Geographers. With the inevitability of becoming President and having to prepare an address for delivery at Lancaster in January 1980, I wanted to choose a topic relevant for colleagues in both physical and human geography, the latter in both its historical and contemporary aspects. Furthermore, I wanted to discuss some real problems, some arenas of active research, rather than enter the hortatory lists to urge colleagues to follow one methodological example rather than another.

It seemed natural to start from my own long-standing interest in regional economic development. Considered on a global scale, patterns of growth and change involve a complex interplay of short-term and long-term problems, and also fascinating issues concerning the significance of natural environmental conditions in relation to the intervention of human agency. Also important is the relative significance of processes endogenous within a nation and the role of exogenous variables mediated through international trade, world financial institutions and other such mechanisms. Given the interdependence of the world economy, attention will be devoted to both the more advanced nations and to the less developed, though primarily in a two-fold context relevant for the less developed economies. One context is the nature of the lessons that can be learned from the experience of the world's core nations which can be applied to the periphery. The other context is the nature of the impact of the core upon the periphery: has it been advantageous or disadvantageous for the peripheral nations?

The writing of this book was made possible by sabbatical leave granted by the University of Cambridge for the Michaelmas Term, 1980, for which I am very grateful. I am also grateful to Mr M.

Young, Department of Geography, Cambridge, for drawing the majority of the illustrations.

Harston, Cambridge
September 1981

1 Introduction

I do not know which makes a man more conservative – to know nothing but the present, or nothing but the past. (Keynes, 1926)

Since the end of the second world war, the volume of literature that has been published concerning the empirical facts of economic growth and development, the concepts that are relevant in analysing the observed patterns, and in attempts to generate theories that will serve to illuminate what is, and what should be, has been vast. What, therefore, can the justification be for yet another book on the subject? Three possible reasons lie to hand, only one of which is relevant in the present context. The first would be to offer new data that had not previously been available, whether for a single region or country, or more generally on a global scale. Second, there might be new theories or concepts to discuss, of a kind that would illuminate existing factual knowledge and possibly lead either to a reinterpretation of the past or to new policy prescriptions for the present. This volume makes no claim to offer either of these. Instead, the justification lies in the third reason. In every generation, it is necessary to examine afresh the existing corpus of empirical knowledge and also the ideas which are current, and those which have been discarded as out-moded, to see whether present conventional attitudes are correct and, if so, to what extent and in what circumstances. The converse is to examine where conventional wisdom is lacking and needs rethinking. In this sense, therefore, the present book has the character of an extended essay in which I offer a viewpoint, grounded in both empirical reality and theories of development, which, I hope, provides a framework within which to think about the wealth and poverty of nations.

Reading what is admittedly only a small sample of the total literature, I have been impressed by the apparent dialogue of the deaf which seems to characterize much writing. This deafness stems from three sets of problems, which to some extent intersect and mutually reinforce each other. First is the temptation to identify explicitly disciplinary boundaries within which to work. This approach leads one to argue the case for 'economic', 'sociological' or 'geographical' causes for differences in wealth between nations and for rates of change over time. In general, this fault appears to have been more prevalent in the 1950s and 1960s than more recently.

The second issue is the differing ideological stance of scholars. At one extreme, in the days of colonial empire it was fashionable to talk of 'the white man's burden'. This Eurocentric view of the world assumed that, but for the 'improvements' wrought by Europeans in Latin America, in Africa and in Asia, the manifest poverty of their peoples would be even worse. Their salvation, so it was thought, lay in emulating their European mentors. Directly opposed to this view is the more recent neo-Marxist argument that the wealth of the more advanced nations has only been achieved by the systematic transfer of resources from the world's poor nations. For example, Caldwell (1977) asserts that 'overdevelopment' has occurred through the transfer of non-renewable (especially energy) resources, and also protein foodstuffs, from the underdeveloped nations, which have been impoverished thereby. Somewhere between these extreme positions is the sense of guilt that motivates many people in the more developed countries to advocate the need for more international aid, a reconstructed world economic system, the abandonment of the arms race, etc. One of the most important examples of this moralistic, humanitarian approach is the report of the Brandt Commission (1980), in which a group of internationally eminent men attempt to stir the conscience of mankind.

The third set of problems arises from a failure to recognize the significance of different time-spans and geographical scales of enquiry. Models of short-term change over a few years have little relevance for changes which occur over decades or even longer, and conversely. Consequently, conclusions drawn in one context are unlikely to be relevant in another. Similarly, much of the literature is singularly aspatial in character and therefore ignores the wide diversity of geographical reality and also the fact that all development processes occur in a spatial dimension as well as a temporal one.

In the pages that follow, I have attempted to break down a few of the barriers to meaningful discourse. Although I myself conceive of the present book as an essay in detached analysis, no doubt readers who are radically inclined will feel that in fact the text is ideologically 'committed' to the defence of the 'capitalist' world order. However, the strategy adopted is essentially that of a dialogue between fact and theory, between short-term and long-term analyses, and between analyses framed on a regional as opposed to a global scale. Ideological issues will be discussed, but are not the central focus of concern. In a sense, I see the present work rather in the manner described by Colin Clark in his 1940 classic *The Conditions of Economic Progress* (p. viii):

> Theory has a valuable, indeed an essential part to play in the development of economic science. But it must be theory which respects facts, not tries to supersede them. There is room for two or three economic theorists in each generation, not more. Only men of transcendental power of reasoning can be candidates for these positions. Re-statements of economic theory, of which we are offered so many, are only occasionally needed, as factual knowledge advances and institutions change.
>
> The rest of us should be economic scientists, content steadily to lay stone on stone in building the structure of ordered knowledge. Instead, it seems to be the ambition of nearly every teacher of economics to put his name to a new formulation of economic theory. The result is a vast output of literature of which, it is safe to say, scarcely a syllable will be read in fifty years' time. But the discovery of new facts, and of generalisations based on them, is work for all time.

I share the view, expressed by Myint (1964) and Supple (1972) among others, that a single model of economic development is, given the multiplicity of real-world circumstances, beyond our reach. As Supple comments: 'If we accept this line of argument it therefore becomes not only permissible but necessary to envisage different sorts of explanatory frameworks for different "types" of economic development....' (p. 34). There is the risk that the number of 'types' of economic development which one recognizes will expand until one is driven to deal with unique cases. This would be a *reductio ad absurdum* just as untenable as the view that a single theory can serve in all cases. A major purpose of the present volume is to explore the middle ground between these polar positions. We will attempt to establish some guidelines for the levels of generalization that are appropriate for specified circumstances, the conditions under which certain processes are dominant. In doing so, it will be necessary to think in terms of broad categories of countries.

A customary feature of contemporary scholarship is to begin a study by appropriately defining the terms and concepts to be employed. I have no quarrel with such a procedure and indeed regard it as a necessary and proper thing to do. However, many concepts are time- and/or space-dependent, with the result than an unequivocal definition is likely to imprison us in the artificial categories that we have specified. Consequently, we are faced with the dilemma, in another guise, which is implicit in the previous paragraph, and it will be helpful to comment briefly on just a few concepts and the way in which their meaning can, and does, vary. For example, by 'income' we conventionally mean a flow of money or useful goods and services. For the purpose of national income accounting, the continuous, circular flow of income can be measured as inputs into the productive system, as the outputs which result, or as consumption. Subject to adjustments for stock changes, savings, etc., all three methods of measuring the national income should yield identical results. Income is differentiated from 'capital' on the one hand, and 'wealth' on the other, both of these terms denoting a stock of (productive) assets rather than a flow of resources. However, a stock of physical assets requires maintenance and replacement. Measured over several decades, and certainly over centuries, the distinction between income and wealth disappears. Similarly, economic 'growth' is usually taken to mean an expansion in total output without any change in the composition thereof. By contrast, 'development' is a term used to signify an evolution of the economic structure accompanying expansion in total output. The former term can only have meaning in a relatively short-term context. By contrast, 'modernization' is generally taken to mean the social transformation of a nation; development necessarily implies some degree of modernization, though modernization may not be accompanied by expansion in total output (economic development). Finally,

It must be recognised that in a long-period analysis the distinction between 'economic' and 'noneconomic' factors loses significance, and it becomes necessary to acknowledge that economic growth must be seen as a special aspect of general social evolution, rather than as a process which can be factored out of the social system and studied in isolation. (Bruton, 1960, pp. 297–8).

The broad facts of recent history are relatively well known, thanks to the expansion of our knowledge about post-war conditions on account of the establishment of reasonably uniform national income accounting procedures. The modernity of this information is something that is easily overlooked. The main pioneering studies were published in the inter-war years, but it was only in the aftermath of the second world war, forcefully prompted by Keynes and the needs of the emergent, formerly colonial, underdeveloped countries, that the United Nations embarked on a systematic programme of annual data collection and publication. In the light of contemporary data and the awakened interest in development processes generally, economic historians have worked over the available proxy variables (employment, personal incomes, output of major industrial sectors, etc.) to compile estimates of national income back into the nineteenth century; such long-term estimates are confined to the presently more highly developed nations of the world, for the obvious reason that it is only for countries like Britain, France, the USA and Japan that adequate historical information exists.

The present-day distribution of income *per caput* is portrayed in Figure 1. With the exception of some oil-rich nations such as Libya, Saudi Arabia and some of the Gulf states, and Australia and New Zealand in the southern hemisphere, the world's wealthiest nations circle the globe in the temperate northern latitudes. By contrast, the poorest countries are all found in Africa and Asia, though in both regions there are some countries with *per caput* incomes in the middle range. Central and South America are striking for the relatively uniform level of *per caput* income, even though the general standard of living is fairly low. In terms of aggregate population inhabiting states with very low personal incomes, the world's problems are concentrated in the Indian subcontinent and Indonesia: India, with a 1978 population of 644 million and an average annual income of US$180; Bangladesh, 85 million and $90; Pakistan with 76 million and $240; and Indonesia with 136 million inhabitants and $340 income per person. The next largest country which is poorer than one of these four nations is Vietnam, whose 52 million citizens live on approximately $160 each, with Burma and Ethiopa as runners up.

There is no doubt that the gap in average incomes between the richer and poorer nations has widened dramatically during the past 200 years. Kahn estimates that prior to 1775, the richest 10 per cent of nations enjoyed personal incomes five times the level obtaining in the world's 10 per cent of poorest countries. By 1875, the gap had widened to a factor of twenty and by 1975 had reached approximately seventy (Kahn, 1979; World Bank, 1976). Kahn expects the gap to widen still further, to about 200 to one in the early twenty-first

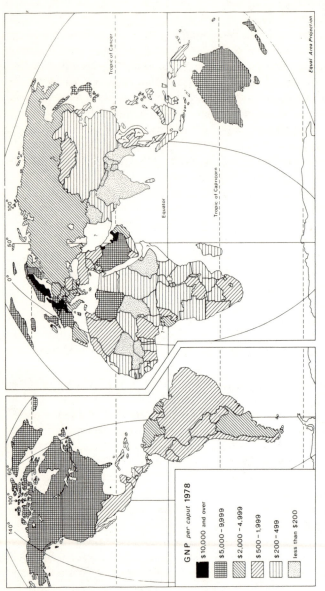

Figure 1 *World distribution of GNP per caput, 1978*
Source: World Bank (1981).

century but expects that thereafter the discrepancies in relative income will begin to narrow. This relatively optimistic view is shared by Leontief and his co-authors (1977) though disputed by others (for example, Freeman and Jahoda, 1978). Whatever the prognosis for the future, nobody doubts the historical fact of a large and widening discrepancy between the income available per person in the world's richest and poorest nations, since the magnitude of the gap is far greater than the possible errors of estimation. Morgenstern (1963) has shown that errors in the estimation of national income may be as large as ± 10 per cent even for an economy as advanced as the USA, and Kravis *et al.* (1978) have examined the additional problems that arise in international comparisons from the choice of the appropri-

Table 1 *Comparison of* per caput *incomes for sixteen nations, using different foreign exchange parities, 1973*

		Income per caput		
Country	Population mid 1970s (thousands)	US dollars converted at official exchange rates	'International' dollars*	Ratio
Kenya	12,480	184	379	2.06
India	577,000	129	394	3.06
Philippines	40,120	259	755	2.91
Korea, Republic of	34,070	366	904	2.47
Colombia	22,500	440	1106	2.51
Malaysia	11,310	633	1180	1.86
Iran	31,410	914	1809	1.98
Hungary	10,430	1619	2793	1.72
Italy	54,910	2525	2913	1.15
Japan	109,100	3738	3962	1.06
United Kingdom	56,020	3136	3750	1.20
Netherlands	13,440	4402	4234	0.96
Belgium	9,740	4618	4663	1.01
France	52,130	4777	4709	0.99
Germany (FR)	61,980	5535	4791	0.87
United States	210,410	6192	6192	1.00

* See p. 18 for a description of the 'international' dollar.

Source: Kravis, *et al.* (1978) table 1.2.

ate exchange rate parity; Table 1 summarizes their findings. An 'international' dollar, as used in the Kravis study, has the same purchasing power over the United States GDP as a whole as does the US dollar, but its purchasing power over individual categories is different because this is determined by the structure of international prices. Consequently, the weighting given to the components of GDP differs from that obtained by the conventional use of official exchange rates. The broad pattern is quite clear, that conventional comparisons tend to exaggerate the gap between the rich and the poor nations by a factor of up to three. When allowance is made for the probably greater under-estimate of incomes in the poorer than in the richer countries, the *per caput* differential is reduced still further, but by no stretch of the imagination is it eliminated.

There is little point in debating the precise magnitude of the income gap, so long as we have enough information to understand its nature and operative mechanisms. For the present it is sufficient to consider what one's attitude to the gap ought to be. At this stage in the present book, I will content myself with quoting a passage from Kahn (1979, pp. 60–2) that summarizes my own viewpoint:

Unlike others who discuss the popular concept of the 'widening gap' between the rich and the poor, we focus on the positive aspects of the gap. The increasing disparity between average incomes in the richest and poorest nations is usually seen as an unalloyed evil to be overcome as rapidly as possible through enlightened policies by the advanced nations and international organizations. If this occurred because the poor were getting poorer, we would agree, but when it occurs at all, it is almost always because the rich are getting richer. This is not necessarily a bad thing for the poor, at least if they compare themselves with their own past or their own present rather than with a mythical theoretical gap. . . .

It is one thing to wish the world were a better place, and quite another to make it happen in the very near future. World leaders who proclaim that closing the gap between the rich and poor countries is the most urgent task of our times should ask themselves how this can be done. This alluring goal simply cannot be approached, much less attained, in the next 100 years.

In Chapter 3, we will return to the key issue posed in the passage quoted from Kahn, namely, the impact of the 'rich' countries on the 'poor', and the extent to which the benefits of development have spread to the less fortunate nations. Meantime, it is useful to note the distribution of the world's *nations* according to Kahn's classification into poor, affluent, etc. (Table 2). The major country in

Table 2 *A classification of the nations of the world, 1978*

Category	Total population (thousand million)	Per caput gross product (US $)
Very poor	0.250	160
Coping poor	1.000	300
Communist Asia	1.000	500
Middle Income	1.000	1000
Affluent Communist	0.333	4000
Affluent Market Oriented	0.667	8000
World	4.250	2000

Source: Kahn (1979), p. 86.

the group 'very poor' is Bangladesh, with a number of African states in addition; likewise, India accounts for a substantial part of the population in the group of 'coping poor' nations. There is no significant country in the world for which there is evidence of an absolute long-term decline in *per caput* income, though world recession, war, famine and other disasters account for short-term reductions in the national income per head in some countries.

Income does not measure the quality of life. On the one hand, average figures conceal wide variations in personal circumstances. On the other, the quality of life is determined by externalities of climate, settlement configuration, availability of leisure resources, etc., of a kind that cannot be purchased through private means alone. In the full recognition of this fact, an essentially hedonistic view will be taken in this book. An increase in product per person implies greater opportunity to provide the good things of life for the population; in general, such an increase may be regarded as a necessary, though not a sufficient, condition for improving the lot of man. In most countries, especially those with a large rural population, the scope for improving the position of ordinary folk by the redistribution of incomes from the rich members of society is limited, and could in any case only effect a once-and-for-all change, whereas the basic need is for sustained increase in output per person across the population at large.

It is well known that modern economic growth began earlier and more vigorously in Britain than elsewhere. If we accept the judgement of Rostow (1978), then the chronology of events may be

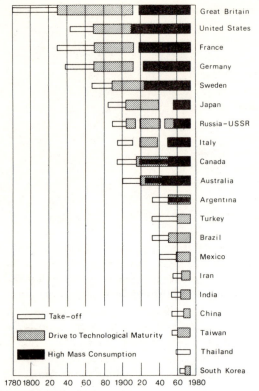

Figure 2   *Stages of economic growth, twenty countries*
Source: Rostow (1978).

portrayed as in Figure 2. Western Europe, North America and Japan are today commonly regarded as the 'core' of the world's economy; if the Soviet bloc plus China is set apart, then the remainder of the world is often described as being the 'periphery'. Indeed, this core/periphery dichotomy is a theme that runs through a great deal of the literature, as we shall see in Chapter 3. For the moment we will not elaborate on this theme, beyond noting the following general points.

Given the historical evidence summarized in Figure 2, there can be no doubt but that the 'core' has expanded to include more nations and an increasing proportion of the world's population. The binary classification of countries into core and periphery is not static and unchanging. This expansion of the core is reflected in Table 2, which shows that nearly 16 per cent of the world's inhabitants live in affluent market-economy countries; if the affluent communist nations are included, then about 24 per cent of mankind is accounted for. Although it would be a gross over-simplification to assert that the growth processes in the core nations will all be similar yet distinct from the processes in peripheral nations, it is reasonable to postulate that the development paths of the two groups are likely to differ: in particular, the balance between endogenous and exogenous processes, mediated in part by the size of nation (size measured in terms of population or national income), is likely to differ, as also is the precise form of both sets of processes. Figure 3 indicates the nature of this *first approximation* to a typology of growth processes, which is proffered with full awareness of the problems to be encountered in ensuring that the boxes portrayed do not remain empty (Clapham, 1922). Furthermore, the distinction between endogenous and exogenous processes should not be taken to imply that they are mutually exclusive; indeed, for every nation there is some relationship between both sets. Also, at this stage in the argument we must keep an open mind regarding the possibility that either or both the endogenous and exogenous processes could be favourable or unfavourable to the development of individual nations or groups thereof.

Associated with development are major structural changes in the economies of nations. The relative shift of resources from primary production (especially agriculture) into manufacturing and service employments is a well-known phenomenon, which was first described in quantitative terms by Clark (1940). Equally familiar are the changes regarding which industry, or group of industries, has played the leading role in development. Textiles, coal, transport,

	Core (developed)		Periphery (developing)		Communist	
	Large	Small	Large	Small	Large	Small
Agricultural economy						
Endogenous growth processes						
Industrial economy						
Exogenous growth processes						

Figure 3   *A first approximation to classifying growth processes*

iron and steel were of prime importance during the early and middle nineteenth century, whereas by the end of the century chemicals and the industries associated with electricity came to the fore in the then developed states, to be followed by automobiles in the twentieth century. The question which remains unresolved is the nature of the *causal* relationship between development and these structural changes.

Above all else, however, is the question: why has development occurred where it has, rapidly in some parts of the world and slowly elsewhere? If it is possible to find an answer, however incomplete, to that question, then it may be possible to form a judgement about the prospects for the less prosperous nations and the time-scale that is relevant in an examination of global development. Such an approach is essentially optimistic, in the sense that I do not subscribe to the belief that the 'finite' nature of the world's resources makes it impossible for the poorer countries to achieve very substantial development. The population explosion appears to be a passing phase of history; one of the more significant events in 1980 was the announcement by the government of China that, whereas in the past encouragement had been given to the increase of population, henceforth there will be official encouragement and help for the control of fertility. This shift of policy should have a material impact on the rate of growth of world population, a growth which already shows signs of staying constant instead of accelerating, as hitherto (see Table 31, p. 146).

The preceding discussion leads me to suggest that in thinking about the development process it is helpful, indeed necessary, to consider *simultaneously* both the geographical scale of analysis and the time-span under consideration. Geographers have for long been aware of the implications of geographical scale, and Haggett's 1964 paper is a classic example of the way in which the scale variable can be handled. Concerned to explain the distribution of residual forest in south-east Brazil, he examined an area of 100 square kilometres and a much larger region, of some 60,000 square kilometres. The variables that can be identified on the one scale differ from those for which data can be collected on the other:

At the *regional* level, multiple regression analysis was used to test five alternative hypotheses and two factors, forest density and terrain ruggedness, were shown to explain over half the distribution. At the *local* level differences in data limited both the hypotheses and the methods of testing them. Multiple variance analysis suggested that terrain was again important as also was accessibility ... the inversion of accessibility as a factor.... (p. 376)

Essentially the same point is valid in the study of history. As Braudel (1972, p. 21), a leading French historian, has commented: 'Distinctions will have to be made between long-term movements and sudden growths, the latter being related to their immediate sources, the former to a long-term span.' Specifically in the context of economic development, Gould (1972, pp. xvi and xvii) has expressed much the same thought:

There is no simple and agreed answer to the question: why have Sweden and Japan experienced a rate of growth of *per capita* income of more than 2 per cent per annum over the past hundred years, whereas Australia has not been able to manage even 1 per cent? ... If explanations of fast and slow growth on a very general level are as yet not widely agreed, there has nevertheless been a great deal of investigation of the relationship between particular factors and economic growth in individual countries and over shorter periods.

The idea stated in the previous paragraph, and exemplified by just three authors, can be generalized as in Figure 4. In principle, there is an infinite number of possible locations in the two-dimensional space identified by the a and b axes. As a consequence, the variety of possible relevant variables and explanatory systems, located along the c axis, is also infinite. In practice, the axes of the three-dimensional space cannot be treated as continuous variables, with the result that the potentially infinite array of points is reduced to a finite number, albeit this is extremely large – too large to be fully comprehended by one person. Much of the apparent conflict of testimony between authors over the nature of growth processes arises from the failure explicitly to recognize that any particular study has a special location in the three-dimensional space of Figure 4, and that the transference of conclusions from one such location to a problem differently located is fraught with difficulty and is often impossible.

This difficulty is increased by the fact that there is a double significance attaching to both the a and b axes. With respect to the time dimension (a), we must also consider when in history the period considered is located. As Gould (1972) emphasizes, the historical period within which a time-span of given duration is located is very

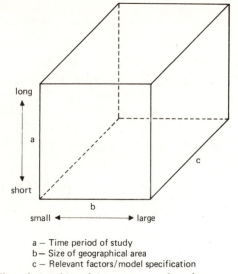

a — Time period of study
b — Size of geographical area
c — Relevant factors/model specification

Figure 4   *The relationship of time, space and explanatory system*

important in the examination of growth processes, for three reasons. The technology available changes over time, the world economy to which a particular nation must accommodate varies, and economic knowledge has expanded, with consequential effects in economic management. As for the b axis, representing size of geographical area, the second construction to be put on this dimension is the nature of the delimited space. Variations in natural endowment and the impact of human intervention both affect the opportunities available to the inhabitants. Figure 4 must be treated as providing a schematic representation of a complex set of relationships; nevertheless, as subsequent chapters will show, the framework sketched is a very useful one within which to think.

This provides a convenient point at which to conclude this introduction. In the chapters that follow, I shall review a number of themes that are relevant to the process of economic development. In so doing, I shall seek to relate theory to empirical reality, so that a dialogue is maintained between real and imagined worlds. Among other things, it is the want of such a dialogue that has rendered much of the literature, whether in the mainstream of theoretical economics or in the 'radical' (Marxist) tradition, a nugatory exercise, at best harmless and at worst misleading.

2 The search for a *primum mobile*

The literature of economics is extensive, our use of it highly selective. Each generation of economists perpetuates what it likes and neglects what it does not. (Routh, 1975, p. 2)

The real world is complex but man tries to simplify it. The process of simplification implies the elimination of variables that impede analysis, or the neglect of interactions with other variables. Explanatory models constructed by these means are tested and in many cases found imperfect or otherwise wanting, and are discarded in favour of newer models. On the accumulating pile of shards, new intellectual edifices are built, frequently in ignorance of the nature of the foundations on which they are constructed. In one sense, this analogy implies a continuity of thought and knowledge. However, as with archaeological studies, the semblance of continuity can mask sharp breaks and discontinuities. As Schumpeter (1954) is at pains to point out, knowledge is frequently 'lost' and rediscovered. He makes the interesting distinction between 'objective' and 'subjective' originality. The former represents the first time that anyone knew the knowledge in question, whereas the latter refers to a situation in which a second person, by the exercise of original scientific procedures, subsequently discovers the same thing, believing it has not been discovered before. Thus, there is considerable reward in digging among the shards as a means of widening our perspective on the present and future.

There is another reason for such an exercise. Whether as a pedagogue, as someone engaged in the process of government, or as a reformer, it is necessary to visualize how the economy works. In particular, it is necessary to have some understanding of the probable impact of particular policies which are actually being put into practice or are proposed. In practice, the instruments which are available by which to effect change are generally rather simple, often downright crude. Given the complexity of real economies, and given the relatively blunt policy instruments available, we are driven to simplify our picture of the economic system. A particularly seductive simplification is to suppose that an economy operates in either a simple linear chain of causality, or as a fairly straightforward albeit multi-causal system, in both cases with a single variable as the dominant one. Students who emphasize the complexity of the growth process tend, almost by definition, to deny the possibility of deliberate change toward desired goals. It is for this reason that the present chapter is called 'The search for a *primum mobile*'. We will examine some of the more important variables that are ranged along the a axis of Figure 4. A substantial part of the discussion will be aspatial in character. This characteristic of the present chapter reflects in part the nature of the relevant literature in economics – economics as a discipline is remarkably aspatial in character – and partly the fact that once we have examined the general nature of selected factors, it will be possible in subsequent chapters to see how they combine in different ways in different situations to produce the variety of economic growth patterns observed worldwide.

Traditional economic analysis identifies three factors of production – land, labour and capital – and seeks an analytical framework that will show the contribution of all three to the production process and also the share each obtains of the output. This tripartite division provides a convenient point of departure for our analysis and it will

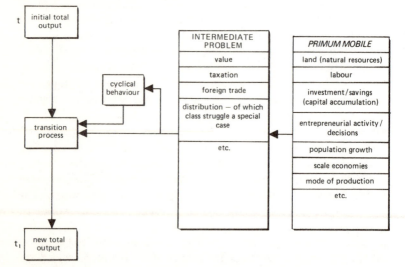

Figure 5   *Schematic representation of economists' approaches to economic growth*

be seen that these three factors occupy the prime position at the top of the list under the heading *primum mobile* in Figure 5. In the history of economic doctrine, land was initially given priority as the factor determining the wealth of a nation, although attention has shifted to other factors and land resources now tend to be neglected. Of the three factors, land is the one most directly associated with geography, and hence the recent neglect of land by economists implies a matching neglect of geographical conditions. For these reasons, it is appropriate to begin with an examination of changing attitudes to land as a factor in development.

Before turning to the consideration of growth, it is helpful to note that interest in this topic has waxed and waned. Classical economists in the tradition of Adam Smith, Malthus, Ricardo and Mill, regarded problems of economic development as of major importance. By the end of the nineteenth century, interest among English-speaking scholars had shifted to other problems – such as economic fluctuations and the distribution of resources among social groups. An important reason for this shift of emphasis was probably that, at least for Britain and the USA, development seemed to be assured in the nineteenth century and was therefore not perceived to be a problem; the position was somewhat different for France and Germany, both of whom were 'catching up' (Arndt, 1978). In addition, as Deane (1978) points out, the triumph of marginal analysis at the end of the nineteenth century, associated with Marshall, directed attention to a whole new set of problems which diverted interest away from growth and development, notwithstanding the fact that Marshall (1890) devoted the whole of Book 4 to that topic. With the major exception of Schumpeter (1949), throughout the twentieth century until after the last world war, only a small number of scholars were interested in problems of development (Arndt, 1978). By contrast, since 1945 the volume of literature on this topic has been truly remarkable. It is important to keep this general point in mind, lest one infer from the passages that follow that interest in growth and development has remained continuously a central concern of economists.

Natural resources, alias land

At first sight, land, labour and capital may be regarded as discrete, separate entities. In practice, the distinctions are blurred, in part because a natural resource rarely has utility without some investment of capital and labour to make it productive (Kindleberger, 1958). For the present purpose, however, it is useful to start with the concept of a natural endowment of climatic, topographic, soil, mineral, etc. resources, such endowment manifestly varying from nation to nation, and being distinct from both capital and labour.

When agriculture was the dominant source of employment, even in the more advanced nations, it was natural to attribute to 'land' the main source of national wealth. Eighteenth-century writers such as Cantillon and Quesnay visualized the economy of a nation as comprising a circular flow of resources among three groups of society – in modern terminology, the landlord class, farmers and providers of manufactures and services. This circular movement of money was initiated, so it was supposed, by the expenditures of the landlords, i.e., from the surplus which had accrued from agriculture (Eagly, 1974). If one reads Adam Smith (1776) closely, it is abundantly clear that he regarded the 'great commerce of every civilised society' to be the trade between a town and its surrounding agricultural area. While he recognized that 'fine manufactures' (for example, silk and high-quality woollens) were dependent upon long-distance trade in raw materials, lower quality manufactures were regarded as based on local supplies of materials. With the nascent industrialization of his time, Adam Smith recognized that commerce and manufactures (and therefore the towns) were the source of innovation and development in agriculture. However, this was, for him, a reversal of the 'natural order of things'. To underline his point, he drew attention to the fast pace of development in North American colonies compared with Europe, the colonies having virtually no manufacturing and depending almost entirely on their abundant land resources. Thus, agriculture was the natural basis of the economy. Hence the national wealth depended on (a) the fertility of the soil and (b) the economic and social organization of the agricultural sector itself, for instance, the system of land tenure.

Just over forty years later, Ricardo (1817) published his major work, which is built upon the concept of rent. As Meier and Baldwin (1957, p. 25) remark:

It should first be noted that Ricardo considers agriculture the most important sector of the economy. The difficulty of providing food for an expanding population serves as the focal point for his entire analysis.

Ricardo and even later classical writers, such as John Stuart Mill, do not appreciate fully the important role that technological progress can play in increasing productivity in agriculture, thereby lessening the difficulty of feeding a growing population.

Ricardo's views were shared by Malthus (1820): 'A fertile soil gives at once the greatest natural capability of wealth that a country can possess' (1951 edn, p. 331).

This 'classical' view of the importance of natural resources as a prime determinant of the wealth of nations was allied to the belief that these resources are finite in quantity and that therefore competition to control them amounted to a zero-sum game. Thus, in the Mercantilist tradition, the possession of overseas colonies was regarded as enhancing the wealth and power of the colonial nation by an amount matched by the diminution of the actual or potential power of rivals and enemies. Notwithstanding the events of the nineteenth century which vitiated this argument, Germany in the twentieth century sought to expand her *lebensraum* and Japan seized an empire in the western Pacific. And since about 1970, the spectre of finite resources which are on the verge of exhaustion has returned (Meadows *et al.*, 1972).

During the nineteenth century and the first three-quarters of the twentieth, several events, or series of events, diverted attention from the natural resource endowment as a factor of importance for the more advanced nations. Adam Smith and Ricardo visualized the growth of an economy as in Figure 6. The initial wealth of a nation,

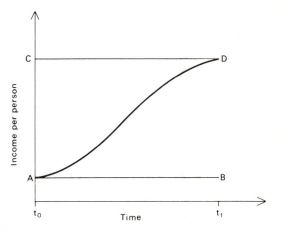

Figure 6   *Economic growth constrained by natural resources*

at a time t_0 and as indicated by AB, is determined by the combination of natural endowment and existing technology. Smith visualized a transition process to a higher income level, CD, which is also set by the finite nature of a nation's resource endowment. Therefore, for Smith the problem of development was the problem of transition from AB to CD. As is well known, Smith emphasized the economies to be had in manufacturing by the division of labour and extension of markets, and by derivation drew attention to capital investment as the engine of change. This was a view that came to dominate thinking about the growth process in the more advanced countries, a domination reinforced by the evidence of increasing returns in manufacturing in contrast to the supposed diminishing returns in agriculture. Hence, Marshall (1890) could observe: 'We say broadly that while the part which nature plays in production shows a tendency to diminishing return, the part which man plays shows a tendency to increasing return' (1949 edn, p. 265). Admittedly, Marshall went on to observe that the two tendencies are constantly operating against each other, but at the time he wrote it seemed clear that the increasing return of man's activities outweighed any tendency to diminishing return from the use of natural resources.

An important reason for this optimistic neglect of land as a factor of production may be found in a whole series of developments that occurred throughout the nineteenth and early twentieth centuries. Improvements in overland and ocean transport opened up very large areas of the world to commerce and settlement. The invention of the cotton gin, barbed wire, grain harvesters, etc., rendered possible the large-scale exploitation of land that was otherwise difficult to use for commercial production. Technological developments in manufacturing industry led to more economical use of raw materials and fuels. Systematic mapping and chance discoveries yielded major mineral finds that in some cases dwarfed the familiar deposits in Europe and the eastern seaboard of North America. Finally, the nineteenth century saw the emergence of Britain's free trade doctrine into the leading, though not the exclusive, principle whereby international trade was regulated. The combined effect of all these developments was to create a situation in which the developed nations (of western Europe and North America) experienced no serious check on account of resource scarcities – though there were periods of relative shortage (Kondratieff, 1935; Rostow, 1978). In terms of Figure 6, the limiting situation imposed by natural resources and represented by CD was lifted so far above the growth path that had been achieved that its actual or potential existence ceased, during the nineteenth and early twentieth centuries, to be a matter for concern.

Thus, the anxiety expressed by Jevons (1865) concerning Britain's future supply of coal proved unfounded. The conservation movement in America, which can be traced back to 1873 and the fear of timber shortages, finding that predictions of resource scarcity were falsified, turned to other aims, especially the preservation of wildlife (Arndt, 1978). The warning by Marshall in 1890 concerning the vulnerability of Britain, were supplies of food and materials to be interrupted, went unheeded at the time; subsequently, steps have been taken to safeguard food and timber supplies, but only against the contingency of war. And in 1962, Kindleberger dismissed fears of materials shortages, on the ground that with much reduced real costs of transport, foreign supplies could and would supplement domestic resources. Thus, in 1957, Meier and Baldwin were distinctly out of fashion in reminding readers of the earlier warnings given by Marshall and Wicksell.

Furthermore, with the process of economic development, major structural changes have occurred in the more advanced nations, manifest in the decline of employment in the primary industries – agriculture, horticulture, forestry, fishing and mining. Associated with this decline in primary employment has been a corresponding reduction in the share of national income originating from this sector. In the case of Britain, the share of agriculture, forestry and fishing fell from about one-third in the early nineteenth century to under 5 per cent at present. Thus, the influence of soil fertility and the quality of resource endowment has become much less important as a direct and readily apparent factor in the more advanced countries.

There is yet another, and perhaps an altogether more fundamental, reason why the contribution of natural resources tends to be ignored. Notwithstanding the assertion by Hirschman (1958, p. 1) that natural resources are 'thoroughly objective, tangible, and quantitative phenomena', climate, soil quality, the value of mineral resources, etc., are not in fact amenable to measurement in terms commensurate with economic accountancy more generally. If we treat land as a form of capital, then the following comment by Clark (1940, p. 374), one of the pioneers of national income accountancy, is highly pertinent:

The tedious and intractable problems of measuring real national income are as child's play in comparison with the difficulties of measuring real national capital. The present writer is by no means alone among the present generation of statisticians in much preferring to keep clear of this problem.

In the case of land drainage and reclamation, large expenditures may be necessary and in this case a capital value can be determined for the new land created. More generally, however, the contribution of environmental quality is manifest in the productivity of the labour and capital applied in its exploitation: consequently the contribution of the land factor is not directly observable.

One solution to this problem of measurement is to assume it away, as indicated by Rostow (1953, p. 64):

It is conventional and often useful to regard the stock of natural resources in an economy as fixed. And there is a sense in which, by definition, they are fixed in nature, exempting geological time periods. Analytically and historically, however, the discovery of natural resources and their effective entrance into the economy can be regarded as part of the economic process, similar to the process of the discovery and application of new techniques.

While this solution has a certain validity for the examination of events over time in one country, to extend the argument and ignore the potential impact of natural resources on inter-country comparisons is stretching credulity too far. The resulting impasse has been vividly described by Georgescu-Roegen (1971, p. 2):

In this representation, the economic process neither induces any qualitative change nor is affected by the qualitative change of the environment into which it is anchored. It is an isolated, self-contained and ahistorical process – a circular flow between production and consumption with no outlets and no inlets, as the elementary textbooks depict it. Economists do speak occasionally of natural resources. Yet the fact remains that, search as one may, in none of the numerous economic models in existence is there a variable standing for nature's perennial contribution. The contact some of these models have with the natural environment is confined to Ricardian land, which is expressly defined as a factor immune to any qualitative change.

And, one might add, apparently invariant in quality from one nation to another. Such an assumption is contrary to the most elementary facts of geography and could only be justified if it can be shown that

Table 3 *Land, labour and capital shares as a percentage of national income for nine nations, 1950–62*

Nation	Land	Labour	Capital, reproducible assets
United Kingdom	2.9	81.1	16.0
United States	3.0	82.0	15.0
Belgium	3.8	78.0	18.2
France	4.2	77.8	18.0
Germany	4.5	74.4	21.1
Norway	4.5	74.2	21.3
Netherlands	4.6	76.4	19.0
Denmark	5.1	78.3	16.6
Italy	6.6	74.2	19.2

Source: Denison (1967), p. 42.

geographical differences are of small moment relative to other considerations. We are not justified in assuming the problem away.

Two distinct approaches to the measurement problem may be identified: attempts to assess the contribution of land either to the total capital stock or income of a nation; and estimates of the land component of international trade. Very few scholars have attempted either approach. Denison (1962 and 1967) is one of the few who has essayed the first. Table 3 reproduces his summary findings for nine nations, the United States plus eight European states. Italy had the highest proportion of its income attributable directly to land, at 6.6 per cent; the lowest proportion, 2.9 per cent, was for Britain. These are all uniformly low proportions. In addition, Denison attempted to estimate how much of the *difference* in national income levels could be attributed to richer or poorer natural endowments. Holding other variables constant, he concluded that the United States enjoyed a *per caput* income approximately 0.5 or 0.6 per cent higher than the European nations because of her relative abundance of land resources. These figures certainly seem to suggest that land is a factor of minor importance. This impression is reinforced by Denison's assumption, when examining the growth of national economies, that land resources remain fixed in quantity. Given that assumption, land makes a zero contribution to the growth of a nation's income and a negative contribution to *per caput* income growth, because of the marked population growth experienced in the sample states between 1950 and 1962. However, these results stem from the assumption made, not from the evidence of empirical findings.

Taken at face value, Denison's findings amply justify the proposition that differences in the level and rate of growth of national income in advanced countries are hardly affected by natural resource endowments. However, such a conclusion is in large measure based on a circular argument to which one is driven by the exigencies of data. In effect, to estimate the significance of land, it is necessary to impute a measure of economic rent. Economic rent arises from locational attributes and from the inherent qualities of the land: in Denison's study, the former predominate over the latter. Such an approach implies that the contribution of land to the national wealth is identified as the surplus product of labour and capital over and above that obtainable from the marginal land employed in the country. Only by making very restrictive assumptions can one conclude that this approach yields a true measure of the land component in the national income, since in practice at least some part of the true contribution will appear as the efficiency of labour and capital (see Furtado, 1964, p. 70). In practice, it seems reasonable to suppose that Denison's estimates represent the *minimum* contribution, and that the significance of land is greater than his estimates would lead us to suppose. As he himself comments:

I know of no attempt to make a comprehensive quantitative comparison of the countries being examined with respect to input of land and natural resources. An adequate effort to do so is quite beyond the capabilities of the present study, but some estimate is unavoidable. (Denison, 1967, p. 183)

Of great interest is evidence that the significance of land as a contributor to national income has been declining. Whereas in 1950–62, land accounted for 3 per cent of national income in the United States, according to Denison (1962), the proportion was 9 per cent early in the present century. One may infer that the same trend has been apparent in Great Britain. Estimates indicate that in 1798 land accounted for 55 per cent of total capital and that this share remained remarkably constant up to 1832 (54.1 per cent) but fell sharply thereafter to 4 per cent in 1927. If Gregory King is to be believed, the proportion had been as high as 64 per cent in 1688

(Deane and Cole, 1967, pp. 270–1). If we consider the wealth of Britain and America one to one and a half centuries ago and compare it with the present-day underdeveloped countries, then the following conclusion seems to be inescapable. Even if, for the modern industrial economies, land is not a major factor in their prosperity, it would appear that its significance for less advanced nations is substantially greater and of an order that cannot be ignored.

The classical economists elaborated a theory of international trade based on the doctrine of comparative advantage. For the purpose of exposition, it was assumed that the productivity of labour was a function of 'natural' factors and, given the assumed international immobility of labour and capital, it is easy to demonstrate that trade will increase the sum of utility available, though less easy to assess how the gains will be shared between the trading parties. The doctrine of comparative advantage led to the view, comfortable for the more advanced nations, that the greatest benefit for *all* nations would be an international division of labour in which the unindustrialized countries continued to export primary produce. This idea was enunciated with brutal clarity by List (1885). He identified stages of development, from savage, through pastoral and agricultural to two further stages, one with agriculture and manufactures, and the highest with commerce in addition. List's views have been summarized by Hoselitz (1960, p. 200); part of his summary is reproduced below:

Whereas all countries have presumably passed through the early stages of development, only the countries in the temperate zone are suited for manufactures. A country of the torrid zone would make a very fatal mistake, should it try to become a manufacturing country. Having received no invitation to that vocation from nature, it will progress more rapidly in riches and civilisation if it continues to exchange its agricultural productions for the manufactured products of the temperate zone.

List's view was widely shared in the nineteenth century, at least among scholars in the more developed nations. There is a remarkable similarity with the attitudes expressed by Le Play, one of the founding fathers of sociology (Brooke, 1970), and by those geographers associated (even if incorrectly) with environmental determinism – for example, Semple (1911) and Huntington (1907 and 1915). There is no need to dwell on environmental determinism in the present context: it was in any case a transient fashion of scholars;

and we shall have occasion to return to the subject in a later chapter (p. 157). But perhaps we should note that this environmental approach to trade explicitly emphasizes the land (natural resource) element of comparative advantage, and hence implicitly stresses land as a factor in the development of countries which are exporters of agricultural and mineral goods.

The twentieth century has seen several developments which have undermined this comfortable Eurocentric picture of the world economy. Discussion of some of these is appropriately reserved to Chapter 3 – notably the problem of the division of the gains from trade and the impact of 'capitalist' economies in 'distorting' the development of the poorer nations. For the present, we note that the theory of trade has evolved in the present century, especially in the 1930s, with the emergence of the Hecksher-Ohlin concept of comparative advantage based on factor proportions (including labour and capital) rather than on land alone. This more sophisticated approach implies that relative advantages are not permanent, and depend at least in part on man-made rather than natural (land) attributes of the productive process. However, the problems of measurement remain intractable, and the *full* evaluation of the factor-proportions theorem – especially the land component – has remained infuriatingly out of reach. The difficulties are nicely illustrated by Vanek (1959) in his attempt to resolve the Leontief paradox, Leontif having apparently shown that the United States exports goods embodying relatively large amounts of labour, whereas one would expect her exports to embody much capital. Vanek's paper clearly shows the problems attending the measurement of the land component of international trade.

The second twentieth century development which has undermined the Eurocentric view of the world, especially since 1945, is the emergence to independence of the former colonial territories. They have sought to emulate the development of the more advanced countries. Conversely, the industrialized states have tried to foster development in the so-called Third World. In this context, therefore, interest has focused on those attributes of the more advanced nations which can be *exported* – technology, education, etc. Attributes of the natural environment, the land, must be taken as given; they have in fact been very largely ignored.

But not entirely ignored. Geographers in the tradition of Gourou (1958) and Ginsburg (1957) continued to emphasize the importance of environmental variables. Particularly in the 1950s, some economists also recognized the significance of these variables (Lewis, 1955; Bauer and Yamey, 1957; Kindleberger, 1958; Myint, 1964; Onyemelukwe, 1974). The qualitative nature of the discussion in these and other works did not fit into the framework of formal economic theorizing which became the vogue after the last world war (summarized by Hahn and Matthews, 1965; and by Wan, 1971). Nor was a qualitative approach appropriate in the elaboration of econometric models, another significant feature of post-war economics. For about two decades, the mainstream of development literature gave scant regard to the widely differing resource endowments of the poorer nations, and ignored the much greater relative importance of these endowments (or lack of them) than has appeared to be the case for the more advanced countries. During this period, industrialization was widely regarded as *the* road to development.

Since about 1970, attitudes have begun to change yet again, placing more emphasis on land resources. Alarmist literature such as Meadows *et al.* (1972) prophesied the end of development on account of the exhaustion of resources and/or intolerable pollution, unless relevant avoiding action were taken quickly. At the end of 1973, the OPEC countries raised the price of oil sharply in the context of the latest (and last?) Israel–Egypt war. Rostow (1978) is of the opinion that from about 1972 the world entered a stage of the Koudratieff cycle in which food and materials become relatively scarce and expensive. Certainly it is interesting that international statistics now differentiate the oil-rich from the other developing nations, thereby recognizing the significance of one major natural resource on the global pattern of development (GATT, 1978). A recent, although rather naïve, example of the re-entry of environmental considerations is provided by Kamarck (1976), who places main emphasis on climate. In many respects, the Foreward by Streeten is more interesting than the book itself, since Streeten, one of the world's leading development economists, draws attention to the rejection of pessimistic environmental determinism following the independence of formerly colonial peoples and makes the point that thereby an important variable, environment, has not been given appropriate attention: 'The focus on climate is necessary only because it has been neglected.'

To summarize the position thus far, it is manifest that the incorporation of land into conventional national income accounting presents enormous problems, perhaps insuperable. It would

Table 4   *A classification of Third World countries*

	Size	Rural population pressure	Primary export range and prospects	Examples
1	small	overpopulated	narrow: unfavourable	Caribbean and Indian Ocean islands
2	small	some pressure	narrow: favourable	Middle East
3	small	some pressure	narrow: unfavourable	the Sahel
4	small	underpopulated	diverse: moderate	most of tropical Africa
5	medium	some pressure	narrow: favourable	the Mahgreb, South-East Asia
6	medium	underpopulated	diverse: favourable	South Africa, Nigeria, Peru
7	large	overpopulated	diverse: varying	South Asia, China

Source: Auty (1979), p. 233.

appear that although land may be a relatively unimportant variable for the more advanced nations today, for the self-same countries it was substantially more significant at stages of development which were quite high by comparison with the present-day poor states. And there are signs of a revival of interest in land as a factor influencing development. Consequently the question arises: how can one incorporate this variable in quantitative analysis of development?

Auty (1979) has elaborated a classification of the less developed countries that was suggested by Myint in 1964. Auty has in fact restricted his concept of resources to those entering the export sector, whereas Myint conceived of natural resources more generally. However, to illustrate the principle, Table 4 reproduces the groupings suggested by Auty. One can readily visualize that the countries in the seven classes may have very different experiences of development. That this is indeed the case has been shown by Chenery in studies that have been published over many years, culminating in two recent books (Chenery and Syrquin, 1975; Chenery, 1979). The earlier study examined the period 1950–70, while the later one deals with the more recent period 1960–75. The basic methodology used is the same in both studies, though the presentation is much more highly technical in the second than in the first.

Recognizing the heterogeneous nature of the developing countries, Chenery seeks to find reasonably homogeneous groups in an attempt to identify those elements of the growth process which are common to all nations, those which are relevant for the classes identified, and those which are specific to individual nations. Data were compiled for over 100 nations, from which an initial classification was made into large countries (those in excess of 15 million population) and small nations. On the basis of foreign trade statistics, the latter subdivide into countries with an orientation to primary industries and those with an emphasis on manufacturing. Given this initial classification, it is possible to identify growth patterns that are 'normal' for each group, i.e., the elements of growth that are common to each group. The next step is to examine the deviations from the norms which have been established and hence to derive a more general typology. For this purpose, Chenery focuses attention on those countries which can be described as 'transitional', excluding both the least developed and most developed economies, and also transitional economies that have been seriously disrupted, mainly on account of wars; very small nations are also excluded. The resulting classification, derived from Chenery's 1979 study, is presented in Table 5.

Of the group identified as specializing in primary products, Chenery and Syrquin (1975, p. 104) say: 'This group corresponds to the established concept of an export-led growth pattern based on favourable primary resources.' By contrast, the twelve nations specializing on industry generally have a rather poor resource base. The majority of the twenty-one nations comprising the group characterized as import substituting and having balanced development, have reasonable or good natural endowments relative to their populations; Brazil, Mexico and South Africa are perhaps the three with the best resources over all.

Although the typology developed by Chenery only imperfectly mirrors the inherent natural resources of the countries considered, his studies mark an important step towards a more sophisticated appreciation of the importance of land in the development process, especially for the less developed nations. However, 'there is no single criterion for classifying countries according to resource endowments that is both statistically feasible and theoretically satisfactory' (Chenery and Taylor, 1968, p. 396).

Table 5 *A classification of development patterns*

Strategy	Population (millions)	GNP per caput, 1965 ($)	GNP per caput, annual average growth rate 1960–75 (%)	Exports per caput, annual average growth rate 1960–75 (%)	Manufactured exports as a percentage of manufacturing production
1 Primary specialization					
Tanzania	12	67	3.0	1.0	18
Nigeria	49	88	3.4	9.5	2
Indonesia	84	105	2.4	9.0	1
Bolivia	4	124	2.5	6.0	1
Sri Lanka	11	142	2.0	−1.0	n.a.
Ivory Coast	4	179	3.5	2.7	24
Zambia	4	179	2.0	−1.2	2
Algeria	12	202	1.8	−1.1	n.a.
Dominican Republic	4	215	3.4	2.6	4
Iran	25	218	8.1	7.9	6
Iraq	8	249	3.3	1.6	n.a.
Malaysia	9	258	4.0	3.1	28
Saudi Arabia	9	271	6.6	11.2	0
Nicaragua	2	330	2.4	4.8	12
Venezuela	9	830	2.2	−1.0	0
Total population	243				
2a Import substitution					
India	481	84	1.3	0.5	8
Ghana	8	156	−0.2	−2.5	n.a.
Ecuador	5	195	3.4	7.9	1
Brazil	81	216	4.3	5.4	5
Colombia	18	228	2.7	0.5	3
Turkey	31	244	4.0	5.1	2
Chile	9	419	1.3	1.3	6
Mexico	43	434	3.2	0.9	3
Uruguay	3	498	0.5	2.0	3
Argentina	22	787	3.1	1.8	2
Total population	700				

Table 5 *continued*

Strategy	Population (millions)	GNP per caput, 1965 ($)	GNP per caput, annual average growth rate 1960–75 (%)	Exports per caput, annual average growth rate 1960–75 (%)	Manufactured exports as a percentage of manufacturing production
2b Balanced development					
Thailand	31	110	4.6	5.4	18
Philippines	32	149	2.5	1.3	6
Syria	5	174	2.2	1.3	8
Morocco	13	179	1.9	1.8	16
El Salvador	3	241	1.8	2.4	22
Guatemala	4	278	2.4	5.2	14
Peru	12	289	2.7	−1.4	24
Costa Rica	2	361	3.4	7.7	13
Jamaica	2	420	3.6	3.1	12
South Africa	18	552	2.3	1.7	13
Spain	32	572	5.7	16.8	8
Greece	9	585	6.6	11.0	7
Ireland	3	815	3.2	6.4	n.a.
Total population	165				
3 Industry specialization					
Kenya	10	96	3.2	2.3	23
Egypt	29	138	1.5	0.4	10
Taiwan	12	201	6.3	19.3	35
Yugoslavia	20	415	5.5	15.5	30
Hong Kong	4	512	6.5	7.3	135
Singapore	2	522	7.6	7.7	n.a.
Pakistan	114	84	3.3	1.8	12
South Korea	28	123	7.1	28.6	23
Tunisia	4	198	4.1	6.2	14
Portugal	9	361	6.9	7.0	32
Lebanon	2	446	3.1	6.7	4
Israel	3	1126	5.2	8.1	21
Total population	237				

Source: Chenery (1979), pp. 30–3.

Capital

In the final analysis, capital cannot be unambiguously distinguished from consumption (see p. 14) and is not a primary component of the economic system (Schumpeter, 1949). Nevertheless, capital has played a central role in the examination of economic development. Probably the main reason for this prominence is the fact that capital investment is a necessary condition for the progress of technology and the expansion of markets, the other two 'causes' of the wealth of nations which appear to have received the most attention (Cairncross, 1962, p. 209). Even if we follow Schumpeter (1949) and Hirschman (1958), and pick out the flow of entrepreneurial decisions as the crucial variable, the implementation of decisions implies capital investment to some degree. Thus, Eagly (1974, p. 3) goes so far as to say: 'According to my reconstruction of classical economics, the analytical structure of classical theory is grounded fundamentally in a single major concept: *capital*.'

In the present context, we will not dwell on the connections between savings and investment and the distinction between liquid capital and capital invested in tangible assets. More relevant for our purpose, we recall that after the time of Ricardo and Malthus, problems of development receded into the background of economists' interests. Not until attempts were made to convert the essentially static analysis of Keynes (1936) into a dynamic model of growth was there a serious attempt to systematize the role of capital in the growth process. The basic identity on which these models are built is:

$$g_w = s/v$$
where g_w = equilibrium growth rate
s = the proportion of income saved
v = the capital–output ratio

In the tradition of Harrod and Domar, much effort has been applied to the elaboration of growth models built upon this foundation, but, even with quite elementary relaxations of assumptions, they are complex in the extreme. Some indication of the difficulties is given by Buttrick (1960). If we visualize a model with three variables, as in the expression $g_w = s/v$, and imagine changes (d) in the variables over a finite period of time (say one year), then the following formulation is possible:

$$dA = f_B dB + f_C dC$$
$$dB = g_A dA + g_C dC$$
$$dC = h_A dA + h_B dB$$

A set of simultaneous equations such as this can only be solved unequivocally if it is possible to control all but one variable, in this case two out of the three. However, a model in this form increases in complexity at a very rapid rate if sectoral disaggregation is introduced and if the assumption of constant returns to scale is relaxed; similarly, any other approach to 'reality' adds greatly to complexity.

This complex literature has been admirably surveyed by Hahn and Matthews (1965), Wan (1971) and Thirlwall (1978). There is therefore no need to pursue the details in the present context. All that we need to note is a fundamental problem, that one of the key variables – savings (assumed equal to investments) – is both an input into the system and an output. In addition, this particular approach, generally relying on constant coefficients, is confined to economic *growth* in the relatively short term and cannot readily incorporate *development* with its changes in economic structure, income distribution, etc. Thus, it is not surprising that Hahn and Matthews (1965, p. 111) came to the following pessimistic conclusion:

It is not difficult to devise a multiplicity of models to fit the 'stylised facts', if these are defined narrowly enough. But for a model to be *directly* useful for the understanding of reality it should be able to do more than this: it should be able to yield testable, non-trivial 'predictions'. Thus it is well established that there have been substantial differences between countries and between periods in rates of growth. It would be difficult to claim that any of the models we have discussed goes far towards explaining these differences or predicting what will happen to them in the future.

Nothwithstanding the conclusion reported above, the 1950s and 1960s was a period during which it was widely believed that the rate of growth of economies could be increased if the level of investment could be raised. In other words, there was the confident belief that western economic systems could be transplanted into the less developed nations through the agency of investment, primarily in the manufacturing sector. Although it is unfair to the author, since his work was misunderstood and misapplied, this optimistic view of the investment/development conditions is closely associated with Rostow (1960).

Rostow suggested that during the take-off into self-sustained growth, the rate of effective investment and savings *may* rise from about 5 per cent to 10 per cent of the national income. He subsequently concluded:

The essence of the transition can be described legitimately as a rise in the rate of investment to a level which regularly, substantially and perceptibly outstrips population growth; although, when this is said, it carries no implication that the rise in investment rate is an ultimate cause. (Rostow, 1960, p. 21)

Indeed, before reaching this conclusion, Rostow specifically drew attention to the fact that a rise in the rate of investment could only occur if there were a 'radical' change in the attitude of the given society towards science, towards the alteration of productive techniques and the associated conditions and methods of work, and towards the taking of risk. Finally, he hastened to add that aggregate investment is in any case a concept of doubtful utility; it is necessary to disaggregate by sector and industry, a point strongly emphasized in a later work (Rostow, 1978).

During the 1960s, two authors in particular published major studies of aggregate growth and the contribution of capital and other inputs thereto (Denison, 1967; Kuznets, 1966 and 1971). Table 6 reproduces some data compiled by Kuznets (1971) from various sources for the period 1950–62, and over the long term as well. If we compare the rate of growth of combined inputs (labour and capital) with the expansion of output per unit input, some striking features are evident. Whereas in the earlier periods, over half of the growth in total output could be attributed to increases in the inputs of labour and capital, in more recent times much the greatest increase has arisen from higher productivity.

The rise in productivity amounts to at least eight-tenths of the rise in per capita product in several countries ... improvements in quality of labor and capital – improvements not caused by any extra input of resources – were responsible for the high rate of growth of per capita product so characteristic of modern economic growth. These 'costless' improvements are connected with the tremendous increase in the stock of useful knowledge, much of it traceable to growth of science viewed as a social institution devoted to the production of new tested and hence potentially useful knowledge. (Kuznets, 1971, pp. 306–7)

While the conclusion to which Kuznets comes must be accepted for

Table 6 *Changes in rates of growth of input and productivity, conventional economic accounting in selected developed countries*

				Rates of growth per year (%)				
	Output (1)	Labour (2)	Capital (3)	Combined Input (4)	Output per unit of input (5)	Population (6)	Output per caput (7)	Ratio of (5) to (7) (8)
A Long-term changes								
United Kingdom, GDP								
1855–1913	1.85	0.74	1.43	0.98	0.83	0.86	0.95	0.87
1925/29–63	1.93	0.82	1.77	1.09	0.83	0.47	1.45	0.57
France, GDP								
1913–66	2.33	−0.50	1.95	0.18	2.15	0.40	1.92	1.12
Norway, GDP								
1879–99	1.72	0.68	1.87	0.93	0.78	0.85	0.86	0.91
1899–1956	2.80	0.25	2.47	0.72	2.07	0.79	1.99	1.04
United States, GNP								
1889–1929	3.70	1.74	3.76	2.43	1.24	1.71	1.96	0.63
1929–57	2.95	0.53	1.01	0.64	2.30	1.24	1.69	1.36
Canada, GNP								
1891–1926	2.96	1.82	2.74	2.02	0.92	1.93	1.01	0.91
1926–56	3.89	0.77	2.86	1.18	2.68	1.70	2.15	1.25
B Changes from 1950 to 1962 (national income)								
United Kingdom	2.38	0.40	2.30	0.82	1.55	0.44	1.93	0.80
France	4.70	0.21	3.43	0.95	3.71	1.00	3.66	1.01
Belgium	3.03	0.45	1.51	0.74	2.27	0.54	2.48	0.92
Netherlands	4.52	0.85	4.00	1.67	2.80	1.29	3.19	0.88
Germany (FR)	7.26	1.71	5.36	2.67	4.47	1.13	6.06	0.74
Denmark	3.36	0.60	3.87	1.41	1.92	0.70	2.64	0.73
Norway	3.47	−0.12	3.44	0.80	2.65	0.91	2.54	1.04
Italy	5.95	0.78	2.50	1.26	4.63	0.60	5.32	0.87
United States	3.36	0.80	3.88	1.46	1.87	1.71	1.62	1.15

Source: Kuznets (1971), p. 74.

the modern advanced economies, it does appear that in the earlier stages of their development greater significance should be attached to the expansion of factor input than is now the case. This may well have implications for the present-day, less developed nations in the earlier stages of their economic progress. Nevertheless, the main conclusion to which Kuznets' data lead is that 'non-conventional' inputs are the prime determinant of growth for the more advanced countries.

However important capital investment may be as a necessary condition for development, the evidence suggests that its role may have been exaggerated. Certainly, the notion that development can be ensured if only the rate of investment can be raised to an appropriate level appears implausible. Anyone who has travelled in Third World countries will have seen plenty of evidence of 'wasted' investment, wasted because the local people do not fully comprehend the vehicles, plant or machinery they use and do not take adequate precautions to maintain it. In some cases, failures in upkeep arise from problems in obtaining spare parts and/or skilled mechanics, but in others the failure lies more deeply, in a lack of understanding of the way in which modern equipment works and must be tended. Yet again, grandiose but ill-conceived projects can use a large amount of capital and generate no permanent development whatever. One of the more famous examples is the groundnut scheme in East Africa after the last world war. Consequently, the 'export' of development from the more advanced to the less developed nations must take place primarily by means other than capital investment, although investment will be called forth thereby. The scepticism expressed by Cairncross (1962) concerning the role of capital in the development process appears to have been fully justified.

Labour

For the present, we will assume that Malthus has been proved wrong. Since his famous essay appeared in 1798, the resource constraint to the simultaneous increase in world population and rise in standard of living has operated only locally and so ineffectually that between 1800 and 1950 world population increased by a factor of about 2.5, an increase that has been accompanied by higher average incomes. Although Malthus may have the last laugh, the indications are that the global population will reach stability sometime in the twenty-first century. On the assumption that the stabilization of the world population will remove the Malthusian spectre, we can concentrate our attention on labour as a factor input, both in terms of its quantity and its quality, as a variable affecting *per caput* incomes.

If there is no change in technology, and if there are still unused natural resources available, an increase in population (labour supply) would result in a larger total output but no increase in *per caput* incomes. With constant technology, there is only one way in which population increase might lead to greater wealth, but such an increase would apply to only one state, or a small number of nations, and would be matched by a corresponding worsening of the position for other nations. If the population of a country grows, then its total military power is enhanced and this enhancement may enable the country to conquer neighbouring or overseas territories and/or control international trade. Under conditions that seemed relevant in the eighteenth century to the Mercantilists, of finite world resources, the expansion of military power would certainly be a way in which Britain or France, America or Russia, could arrogate to itself a larger share of the world's wealth. In the eighteenth century, some countries, for example Spain and what is now Germany, experienced an actual decline in population. Not surprisingly, the view was widely held that population increase was a 'good thing'; Colbert translated this view into practical policies of state in France. Out of the discussion around this issue arose an ill-formed concept that a larger population conferred other benefits, in the guise of what we would now call 'increasing returns' (Schumpeter, 1954), an idea that we shall wish to explore later (p. 52).

Another approach to population growth and consequential expansion in the supply of labour has been advanced by Boserup (1965) in particular. Her basic thesis is that an increase in population creates a larger demand for foodstuffs and this in turn stimulates changes in agriculture. The particular change she identifies is the greater frequency with which individual plots of land are used, starting with the shortening of the fallow in shifting cultivation and ending with the multiple cropping of land in each season. Arising from the need to raise food output and the frequency of cropping, technical change in implements and techniques generally is induced. As Grigg (1979) points out, this process of development is almost certainly limited to a small number of societies, since as a theory it makes very restrictive assumptions. However, there are circumstances in which a mechanism resembling Boserup's model does seem to have operated. There is general agreement that between about 1550 and 1650, the population of Holland doubled (Slicher van Bath, 1963; Glamann, 1971 and 1977); according to de Vries (1974), the total rose from 275,000 in 1514 to 671,000 in 1622, which is rather more than a doubling in just over one century. While the reason for this sudden multiplication of people is difficult to ascertain, the effects are not in doubt. The demand for food rose sharply, not only to feed the people but also to maintain the horses used in local transport. Four responses were possible to the greater demand for farm produce and the Dutch pursued all of them. The land area was extended by embankment and drainage. New methods of farming became common – crop rotations, use of legumes, improved implements, etc. – leading to more intensive agriculture. To the extent that increased domestic output was insufficient, imports of grain and livestock rose in relative and absolute importance. And finally, as part of the expansion of commerce, land was converted to flax production to supply the raw material for textile exports.

In response to rising population, at a time when transport systems were poor by modern standards, a revolution occurred in farming practices. First experienced in Holland, the changes spread throughout much of Western Europe in response to similar combinations of circumstances. But the Dutch experience between 1550 and 1650 seems to be the most dramatic case recorded of a growth process that approximates to the model advanced by Boserup.

While historical examples illuminate the present they cannot give clear guidance in the solution of contemporary problems. In any case, the Dutch case provides evidence for the effect of an increase in population, and hence in total demand, rather than an increase in labour supply or a change in its characteristics. Therefore it is appropriate to turn to the evidence of western econometric studies. In the present context, the single most useful of these was published by Denison in 1967. According to his estimates, some of which are incorporated in the tabulation made by Kuznets and presented as Table 6, the *total* contribution of labour to national income rose in all nine countries studied, including Norway. Most of the labour effect, however, was attributable to a larger workforce, though this expansion was offset somewhat by a reduction in annual hours worked and changes in the age–sex composition of the workforce. In addition, improved education and training also added to national income. Only in Belgium, France and Norway did the qualitative aspect of the labour force contribute more than half of the labour effect. If we group the countries studied by Denison according to the contribution of education to the annual rate of growth in national income over the period 1950–62, the pattern is as follows:

0.40–0.44 per cent	0.30–0.39 per cent	0.20–0.29 per cent	0.10–0.19 per cent
United States	—	France	Denmark
Belgium		Netherlands	Germany
Italy		Norway	
		United Kingdom	

In a context of over-all growth rates of 2–3 per cent per annum or higher, the contribution of qualitative changes in the labour force is evidently rather small. In the absence of migration – i.e., the transfer of trained personnel – it is the element of qualitative change that is potentially 'exportable', in the sense that programmes of education and training can be organized internationally. Denison's findings might be construed to suggest that the contribution to be made to the growth of the less developed countries by this means may be small. However, judged by world standards, the nine countries he studied are all highly developed with well-educated populations. It is perfectly possible, therefore, that the marginal gain from additional education is small. By contrast, for countries where development has not progressed very far, and where basic literacy may be very low, the marginal gain from additional education and training is almost certainly very high. Therefore, Denison's estimates, which seem to be reasonable for developed countries, may be used as a guide to the minimum likely relative significance in the context of the poorer nations of the world.

The conventions of national income accounting are probably perverse, certainly for the world's poorer nations. Education is treated as a form of consumption, not of investment. While this may be valid for the richer countries – and Kuznets (1971) is among those who do not agree that it is – it is certainly not very logical for the poorer nations. Precisely the same may be said of health. There is no doubt that the incidence of debilitating diseases and premature mortality in the poorer countries is a major factor leading to low over-all productivity; disease debilities must also contribute to people's unwillingness to innovate. One difficulty, of course, is that health improvement has historically been associated with increased fertility, which in the Indian sub-continent and elsewhere has resulted in such a rapid growth of population that the gains in output from all sources have been severely tested even to maintain the very modest rise in living standards that has been achieved. As with capital investment, improved education and health are necessary conditions for development, but cannot be described as other than the proximate causes thereof.

In the German tradition of economic thinking the triad of land, labour and capital was regarded as inadequate and the role of the entrepreneur ('Unterehmer') was recognized. This fourth concept did not reach the English-language tradition until the time of Mill and through his writing (Schumpeter, 1954), and was not fully developed until Schumpeter's first major work in 1911. Hirschman (1958) put the entrepreneur, and more particularly the flow of decisions, at the centre of the development stage. As commonly conceived, the entrepreneur is distinct from the capitalist, who owns capital, and the mass of ordinary workers, i.e., labour. To the present author, this seems to be a misconceived and artificial distinction. Anyone who is at all familiar with the less developed countries of the world will know that even in the most traditional societies there is much entrepreneurial activity by people whose main livelihood is derived from the land. Although major projects require the services of full-time, highly committed and skilled entrepreneurs, the diffusion of development throughout a society depends on the action of myriad small-time entrepreneurs. Therefore, there is an almost complete continuum, whereby at one end of the scale entrepreneurs are effectively the owners of capital and at the other they have little but their labour to sell. There are many more of the latter than of the former, and therefore it is hard, nigh impossible, to distinguish the entrepreneurial category from the more general social matrix in which it is embedded. Except in the context of major projects – for example transport infrastructure, manufacturing facilities, mineral exploration and exploitation – entrepreneurial ability is not something that can be 'exported' from the more advanced to the less developed nations. This is not to deny the importance of major projects such as the Volta river hydro-electric development, but merely to argue that to emphasize the entrepreneurial group in society is really to shift the problem to the much more general structure of society.

There is one final aspect of labour which must be touched upon. Embedded in the history of economics is the problem of what it is that confers value upon goods, and at one time it was widely held that the labour input was the sole determinant of value. In mainstream economics, the labour theory of value was displaced by a more sophisticated concept, which avoids the tortuous reasoning involved in, among other things, the distinction between use value and exchange value. However, Marx and his disciples have kept alive the antiquated labour theory of value, dressed it up and put it to use. In doing so, the concepts of 'productive' and 'unproductive' activities have also been retained. In his *Principles of Political Economy* of 1848, Mill regarded wealth as the stock of money, bullion and useful goods. By definition, 'productive' labour is that which, either directly or indirectly, adds to the stock of wealth. Likewise, 'productive' consumption is that consumption which is necessary to maintain the productive workers. All other activities and consumption were classed by Mill as 'unproductive'. Mill was careful to point out that, as defined, 'unproductive' work included all that employment which produced ephemeral pleasures, whether artistic or hedonistic in nature, and explicitly stated that such employment should not be regarded as any less important than the so-called 'productive' labour. However, rather carelessly Mill appeared to equate productive and unproductive consumption with social class. Marx and his followers ignore the careful qualifications of Mill, assume that labour is the source of all value, insist on the binary distinction between productive workers and unproductive appropriators, and erect on these quicksands an elaborate edifice of argument and assertion. There are four major difficulties that the present author has with this approach.

1 Although human agency is essential for the creation of value, it seems illogical to deny that the quality and quantity of natural resources have a role to play.
2 To treat capital as embodied labour is fallacious, if only for the reason given in 1 above.
3 The concept of labour input involves nice calculation about the qualities of the various skills and I am not persuaded that they are commensurable, other than through the working of the labour market and the going wage rates.
4 The distinction between use value and exchange value runs into exactly the same problems of measurement that are incurred in welfare economics of estimating consumer surplus.

With these comments in mind, the concept of 'unequal exchange' becomes tenuous and unhelpful. This particular concept is one that is prominent in the Marxist literature on international development, and is something to which we shall return in Chapter 3 (p. 70).

Unfortunately, Marxist polemic has tended to overshadow the classical and neo-classical concern with the health and skills of the workforce. Marshall (1890) devoted Book 4 to the problems of development; three of the six chapters discuss aspects of labour – total numbers, the health and strength of the population, and industrial training. Although this tradition lived on into the post-second world war period (for example, Lewis, 1955; Kindleberger, 1958), with the coming of the 1960s and 1970s it has dropped out of favour. There is little doubt that the desire to regard economic growth as 'exportable' from the more advanced to the less advanced nations, allied to the ideological overtones of the debate, has been a major reason for this neglect.

Economies of scale

As Kaldor (1967) notes, the concept of increasing return, as it was initially known, has a long and distinguished history as a factor in the growth process, a history traceable to Adam Smith. In fact, the concept, albeit in a rudimentary form, had been formulated even earlier, by Petty in 1662 and Serra in 1613 (Schumpeter, 1954), and by the fourteenth-century Arab philosopher–historian, Ibn Kaldun (Clark, 1967). There are in fact three separable but closely related ideas. The first, as formulated by Petty, has been summarized by Schumpeter (1954, p. 258) as follows:

Expenditure on what may be termed social overhead – expenditure on government, roads, schools, and so on – does not, other things being equal, increase proportionally with population. This put increasing returns into the not quite equivalent form of decreasing cost per unit of service.

The second variant, foreshadowed by Serra, is associated with Adam Smith and Marshall. Economies of scale are obtained by firms as the volume of their sales increases. Such expansion permits the spreading of fixed costs over more units of output. In addition, the work processes can be divided into specialist jobs, at which the workers achieve great dexterity; specially devised machinery may replace manual work and raise efficiency even further. In addition, within quite wide limits, a larger machine is proportionately cheaper and more economical than an equivalent one of smaller capacity. (For an admirable exposition of these and other sources of scale economies in manufacturing, see Robinson, 1931.) Economies of scale can be achieved either internally within the firm, or externally through the geographical propinquity of specialized producers. In Marshall's terminology, the trend to 'massive production' must be considered a major stimulus to economic development (Youngson, 1959). But, as Young (1928) cogently argued, it is not necessarily the case that individual production units become larger; the variable of crucial importance is the simplification and mechanization of individual processes or operations. In many circumstances, producing units can be quite small, albeit highly specialized.

Third is the more general case of the increase in both market and non-market aspects of welfare which accrue to the whole population through the expansion of the economy – including, thereby, the availability of education, medical services, etc. – and which in turn has a positive impact on the productivity of the economy as a whole. This much more generalized concept of scale economies, intellectually associated with the welfare economics of Pigou and Meade, is, virtually by definition, almost impossible to quantify.

Probably the first major attempt to examine these ideas empirically at the level of a whole nation was that of Jones (1933). He compiled data for four industries in a major region which, by inference, could be taken as representative of the national structure for the industry in question; his fifth case study was the entire pig-iron industry in the United States:

London building industry	1845–1913
Lancashire cotton industry	1845–1913
Cleveland (England) pig-iron industry	1883–1925
Massachusetts cotton industry	1845–1920
American pig-iron industry	1883–1925

In each case Jones was able to show beyond doubt that over time productivity rose appreciably, and apparently more rapidly in the United States than in Britain. However, his ascription of these productivity gains to the increasing size of the industries, and hence long-term industry economies of scale, is questionable. To show the connection, he uses the ratio and productivity gain to the expansion of the industry as measured by output, finding that the ratios are larger the more rapid the growth. Such a relationship will arise from innumerable causes, of which industry size is only one, and

Jones was not able to test these possibilities.

The International Economic Association, meeting in 1957, examined various evidence concerning the economic implications of the size of nations. The approach can be broadly construed as cross-section in nature, comparing the experience of many countries, rather than historically examining a single nation. In his introduction, Robinson (1960, pp. xviii–xix) attempts to summarize the proceedings thus:

> It would not be easy, or indeed fair to the variety of opinions held by participants, to try to establish any quantitative conclusions from this part of our discussions. It is not going too far, perhaps, to say that it seemed to be our general impression that most of the major industrial economies of scale could be achieved by a relatively high income nation of 50 million; that nations of 10–15 million were probably too small to get all the technical economies available; that the industrial economies of scale beyond a size of 50 million were mainly those that derive from a change in the character of competition and of specialisation – a change which may, if one relies on the contrasts between American and other experience, be explained partly by scale, but may also be attributed to differences of national outlook and to differences in the legal handling of the problems of monopoly, as well as to differences consequent on income and expenditure per head, and due, in part at least, to a richer endowment of natural resources.

To compound the difficulty of assessment, Robinson and the conference participants clearly recognized that trade or other economic associations between nations may allow even quite small countries to gain the advantages of large-scale production while nevertheless retaining their political identity. Furthermore, not one of the contributors considered the potential effect of the spatial arrangement of a given population; a small total population at a high density may be equivalent to a larger total scattered at low density. Nevertheless, the considered view expressed by Robinson suggests that scale economies really may be a significant factor inducing development.

A passionate belief in the beneficial effects of larger scale production is displayed by Clark (1967). He argues the virtues of an increasing population as the means to more economical production and use of resources, both in agriculture and in industry, and thereby as the basic stimulus to development. Unfortunately, the empirical evidence which he marshals is unconvincing and at best can be interpreted as consistent with his proposition. Similarly unconvincing as a *general* explanation of agricultural improvement is Boserup's (1965) thesis that population growth compels the more frequent use of each plot of land, and changes in technology, leading from simple shifting cultivation to densely settled agrarian regions with a complement of specialized services (for example, education and blacksmiths) and associated permanent settlements. While there is a substantial element of truth in this thesis, it is open to serious criticism at both the theoretical and empirical levels (Grigg, 1979). In particular, Boserup's contention is really only applicable at the earlier stages of development and under the assumption of a high preference for leisure. In more advanced economies, other explanations may be more relevant, as discussed in Chapter 3.

Perhaps the most thoughtful studies of scale economies in the development process are two by Youngson (1959 and 1967). In the first of these works, Youngson reviews the variety of ideas which previous authors have offered to explain economic growth and, without falling into the trap of uni-causal explanation, nevertheless puts the main emphasis on economies of scale (both internal and external). Consequently, the widening of markets is crucial, and hence the role of transport improvements in making possible trade over expanding geographical areas. 'The essence of the argument is that cheap transport is the first requirement of economic progress' (Youngson, 1959, p. 48). Around this theme, but including many other stimuli to development, he then proceeds to the study of Great Britain (1750–1800), Sweden (1850–80), Denmark (1865–1900) and the southern United States (1829–54). In each case, the benefits of an enlarged scale of activities – scale economies of all kinds – are apparent, as is the crucial role of improved transport in making these scale economies possible.

In his 1967 study of overhead capital, Youngson distinguishes four main categories: transport; power and irrigation; education (including research); and housing. He notes how the nature and scale of such overhead capital is closely tied to the conditions of the natural environment, and makes the following comparison between the nations which are today developed and those which are described as underdeveloped:

Thus, it must be recognised that the physical resources – the physical economic potential, so to speak – of many underdeveloped countries cannot be utilised until a much greater investment in public assets of the kind we have been discussing has been made than had to be made, relative to available capital, in the case of almost all the countries which are today highly developed. In the case of the latter, only a moderate investment in transport, power supply, irrigation – and an investment which could proceed by modest increments – was necessary for their economic potential to begin to become realisable. In the case of the present-day under-developed countries it is not so. There is for them a difficult threshold to cross, by means of large scale public investment, before general exploitation of resources can take place. Thus the idea of overhead capital is peculiarly relevant to the needs of these countries, not simply because they are poor, or because it is wished to develop them comparatively rapidly, but also because of the physical background of their poverty. Fortunately, these countries, coming forward inevitably later in the history of economic development, can draw upon an unprecedented store of scientific know-ledge. Radical alteration of the environment is no longer impossible. (Youngson, 1967, pp. 113–14).

As examples of large-scale projects which require immense capital resources relative to the relevant underdeveloped economy, Young-son cites the Volta, Aswan and Kariba dams. Though less spectacu-lar, it is equally relevant to note road investment, railways and ports, all of which must often be massive in scale at a very early stage in the development of the present-day underdeveloped nations.

To the extent that increasing returns do operate, they are geographically located in some countries but not in others. More precisely, there is presumably some threshold of development at which increasing returns begin to operate. Thereafter, the continued impact of increasing returns should result in the acceleration of economic change and rising income levels, an acceleration which can be expected to last not just for a few years but for decades, possibly centuries.

Science and technology

If the long span of history is to be divided into epochs which are characterized by quite specific and identifiable processes of growth, then there is no doubt that the modern era is characterized by 'the extended application of science to problems of economic produc-tion' (Kuznets, 1966, p. 9). It is impossible to put a precise date to the beginning of the present epoch. Many of the great inventions and discoveries of the industrial revolution were empirically derived, often by men of quite humble background and occupation, who took the trouble to think about what they were doing and how the equipment in their charge could be improved. Other discoveries, such as Abraham Darby's use of coal for smelting iron, resulted from laborious trial-and-error experiments, not from the application of scientific principles to the solution of a recognized problem. The first major invention to be based on the careful application of science was Watts' revolutionary development of the steam engine. Nevertheless, even until the mid nineteenth century, much industrial development remained essentially pragmatic in nature, based upon the improvement of existing practices. Then, with the introduction of Bessemer's ideas for steel manufacture (1856), the Thomas-Gilchrist technique introduced in 1879, and the basic open-hearth process perfected in 1884, the making of steel on a large scale was revolutionized. Towards the end of the century, the advent of electricity, the internal combustion engine and rapid changes in the chemical industry marked the clear, and irreversible, supremacy of science-based technical development. At the very least, therefore, the modern epoch has lasted for just over one century; on a more relaxed definition, we could say that it has barely extended over two centuries.

The growth of scientific and technical activity implies that there is a stock of knowledge available for all mankind. Rostow (1953) regards this knowledge as a 'free' good available to developed and underdeveloped nations alike. However, some minimal level of scientific and technical accomplishment is necessary before access to this store of knowledge is possible. Therefore, it is more realistic to suggest that the common stock of scientific knowledge is available to all countries at a very low marginal cost; the cost is low compared with the cost that would be incurred to create the knowledge from scratch. For the more advanced nations, continued development requires the sustained discovery of new scientific knowledge and, perhaps more important, the rapid application thereof to all aspects of the economy. For less advanced countries, development will depend on the diffusion of existing knowledge from the core nations. At least, this is a proposition which we can treat as a first approximation; as we shall see in Chapter 5, this is an over-simple view of development in many of the world's poorer nations. The second implication of the growth of science is that a new and autonomous factor has been introduced into the growth process. New discoveries open new opportunities, either to do old things in new ways, or to do entirely new things. Such opportunities create the circumstances for profitable investment, which implies either that competitors are driven out of business or themselves must innovate. For all of the more advanced nations, there is now an inexorable logic that, because scientific knowledge is expanding, the penalty for failure to innovate is a reduction in the standard of living. In the future, there may be diminishing returns to investment in science, but of this there is as yet little sign. For our purpose, it is useful to reckon that within the last 100, or at most 200 years, a new factor of the utmost importance has entered the international stage, and no nation can escape its influence.

Conclusion

We have reviewed a number of ideas concerning the source of economic development, treating each as a potential *primum mobile*. Comparing the concepts – of land, capital, labour, scale economies and technological innovation – with relevant empirical data, we have seen that none can qualify as *the* cause of economic change. This essentially negative and surprise-free finding does have some utility, because we have also taken a few tentative steps towards the recognition of the variable balance of the operative factors according as development is in the early stages or has proceeded for many decades, even centuries. For the most developed nations, land resources and capital appear to be unimportant compared with technological innovation and the ability of the population to accept new ways of doing things. For the poorer nations of the world, the natural resource endowment appears to be much more important at their present stage of development; and investment in basic infrastructure and also in improving the quality of the population (education and health) must have a high priority if sustained development is to occur. In a tentative manner, we have begun to identify a useful dichotomy which will be amplified and explored in the next chapter in terms of the world's core and periphery.

3 Core and periphery

Well before 1900, the widening circle of economic development had transmuted the economies of other important countries. (Supple, 1963, p.39)

Until relatively recently, it was common to think of economic development as occurring in stages, with the less advanced nations following in the footsteps of the more developed. This implausible view of the development process was explicitly rejected by Meier and Baldwin (1957). They proposed a pattern at which we have hinted in Chapter 2. They viewed England as the initial industrial core of the world economy. Her requirements for food and raw materials on the one hand, and markets for the produce of her mines and factories on the other, created a system of world-wide trade whereby economic development spread to other nations. This core–periphery model, which was not original in concept, was elaborated by Wallerstein in 1974. He proposed a tripartite terminology. The initial core is conceived to comprise Western Europe, including Britain. The rest of the world is then categorized as either 'periphery' or 'external arena'. In this terminology, the periphery is that part of the world which is closely linked functionally with the core to supply daily necessities – primarily food and industrial raw materials. The external arena supplies to the core precious goods and rareties, such as spices and silk goods in centuries gone by. Whereas trade is important for the economies of the peripheral countries, it is generally of small moment for the nations of the external arena. In practice, the distinction between periphery and external arena can be hard to make and we will content ourselves with the simple terminology of core and periphery. However, whatever the terms used, it is important to recognize that the categories include countries of widely differing characteristics – by no stretch of the imagination are the members of the categories homogeneous. Furthermore, the fact that a country may be assigned to one category at a particular period in history does not imply that it must stay so classed for ever. Indeed, viewed in the long run, the core has expanded to incorporate an increasing proportion of the world. It is the expansion of the core and the nature of its impact on the periphery which forms the focus of this chapter.

Table 7 summarizes available estimates of the importance of selected countries and regions in world trade. Britain is commonly regarded as the first core nation in the modern era; nevertheless, the

Table 7   *The percentage distribution of world trade, by country and region, 1720–1971*

Country/region	1720	1800	1901–5	1948	1971
Great Britain	13	33	16	12	7
France	8	9	7	5	6
Germany	9	10	12	2	10
Switzerland	1	1	2	2	2
Holland and Belgium	5	4	11	6	8
Scandinavia	2	1	3	6	5
Italy	4	3	3	2	4
Western Europe	42	61	55	35	42
Spain	12	3	2	1	1
Portugal	2	1	—	—	—
Austrian Empire (Austria)	2	2	4	—	1
Turkish Empire	2	1	—	—	—
Eastern (communist) Europe	—	—	—	5	9
of which Russia (USSR)	9	9	4	2	4
Total Europe	69	77	65	41	53
North America	—	—	13	22	18
of which USA	—	5	11	16	13
Canada	—	—	2	5	5
Latin America	12	7	—	12	6
Asia	—	—	—	13	15
of which Japan	—	—	—	0.8	6.2
India	11	3	—	2.6	0.6
Total above	92	92	78	88	92
Various	8	8	22	12	8
Total	100	100	100	100	100

Source: Adapted from Rostow (1978), pp. 70–3.

rest of Western Europe in 1800 accounted for nearly the same proportion of world trade as did Great Britain. Since that time, North America has emerged as another major focus for trade, while Latin America and Asia have collectively had a mixed experience during the two and a half centuries covered by the table. Very striking is the decline of both Spain and India in relative importance, and the recent emergence of Japan.

There is little point in trying to put precise dates to the emergence of particular nations as members of the core group, and the broad outline of the history is well enough known (see Figure 2, p. 20). Western Europe, with Britain in particular, emerged as the first major focus of economic activity with world-wide influence, a position achieved prior to, but then consolidated by, the industrial revolution. With the ending of the American civil war and the completion of the first transcontinental railway link in 1869, the United States developed very rapidly and by the end of the century was well established as a major economy. The travail of the Russian people began to bear fruit only after the first world war, and the impact of her development has been confined primarily to the nations of the communist bloc of countries after the second world war. As for Japan, the accession of Mutsu Hito as emperor in 1867 (the Meiji Restoration) set in train an astonishing sequence of events whereby within fifty years she had made her mark on neighbouring nations, and within a century had emerged as a technologically leading nation of major significance in the world's economy.

Numerous other countries have achieved high standards of living but are not regarded as members of the core group. Australia and New Zealand are two examples. Their populations are small, at about 16 million and 3 million respectively. In addition, although using advanced technology, the small size of their economies precludes them from making a major contribution to scientific and technological advancement, except in limited and highly specialized fields.

Two essentially contrary views are held regarding the impact of the core nations upon the rest of the world. The first is that the development of the richer nations has, in general, been beneficial for the poorer. In opposition is the view that the poverty of the poorer nations has been caused by the richer countries, which have derived an unequal and unfair share of the benefits of global progress. We will examine this second view first, largely to show that it cannot be sustained as a general proposition, though manifestly there are particular cases where the impact of the core nation(s) has been adverse.

Colonialism/imperialism

The last two decades of the nineteenth century witnessed an unprecedented burst of colonial activity in Africa and in Asia. The major European powers, the United States and, early in the twentieth century, Japan, vied with each other in the acquisition of colonies. In one interpretation, this may be regarded as a response to circumstances in the advanced countries, primarily in Europe. As the nineteenth century progressed, international trade in manufactures had become more competitive. The 1870s was a period of recession and, as a defensive measure, several European states imposed import tariffs towards the end of the century, while America and Russia raised their levels of protection. *Prima facie*, the drive to obtain colonies could be interpreted as a strategy for safeguarding markets and raw material supplies, in defence of the national interest of the respective colonial powers.

This Eurocentric view of the period from about 1880 has been carefully examined by Fieldhouse (1973) and found to be wanting. Nor can an adequate explanation be found in non-economic, Eurocentred events such as the rivalries of the main ruling houses. The reality appears to have been much more complicated and to have been conditioned by events, especially in Africa and Asia, occurring far from Europe's shores. Two issues, among the many, are of special interest to us, and both were discussed by Fieldhouse; his work therefore provides a convenient point from which to start.

Detailed evidence on the trade experience of Britain, France and Germany during the last quarter of the nineteenth century does not indicate that colonies were of great importance in the trade of metropolitan powers. Nor does the chronology of tariff changes fit the trade thesis, while evidence for a conscious link between trade and colonialism on the part of European statesmen is lacking, at least in the early years of colonial expansion. In the light of this evidence, and of selected case studies, Fieldhouse concludes that trade considerations were not a major factor until the 1890s, by which time the burst of colonial activity was already well under way. The need to find new markets and safeguard old ones does not appear to have been the cause of Europe's colonial expansion. Nor does the monopolization of trade appear to have been a major effect of the acquisition of colonies. After the system had settled down following the upheavals of the first world war, and at a time of world-wide recession and trade protection in the 1930s, the share of the trade that colonial dependencies conducted with the respective metropolitan powers varied remarkably (Table 8). The need to organize trade clearly was not a *general* explanation, or consequence, of colonial expansion, although important in particular cases; perhaps the most striking of these was Japan's organization of Taiwan to supply rice specially suited to the Japanese palate. Conversely, from about 1895 onwards, British governments, having finally been persuaded of the potential advantages of colonies in the early 1890s, did very little indeed in respect of trade with them (Hynes, 1979).

The imperialism of capital is a separate argument. Ever since the days of Adam Smith, the concept of long-term diminishing returns to both land and capital has been deeply embedded in economic literature. This concept is the basis for Lenin's view that as the capitalist system evolves there will be a steady accumulation of

Table 8 *The trade of colonies with their respective metropolitan countries, 1933*

Colonies	Total exports of colonies (%)	Total imports of colonies (%)
Japanese mandate	97.0	94.9
United States dependencies*	96.6	80.2
Japanese colonies	88.5	83.1
Belgian Congo	71.1	43.4
French colonies	75.0	66.7
Belgian mandate	75.0	16.3
German colonial Empire (1912)	68.3	62.1
Italian colonies	65.5	59.3
Portuguese colonies	49.5	43.0
French mandates	46.1	56.4
British colonies	32.5	24.4
British mandates	31.4	17.9
Netherlands India	17.6	11.9

* Including the Philippines.

Source: Royal Institute of International Affairs (1937), pp. 294–5.

capital, especially in the hands of 'monopoly finance capitalists', and that as a result there will be downward pressure on the rate of profit. Hobson (1948) advanced this argument, as did Hilferding (1970). Hobson expressed the opinion that the downward pressure on profits occurred because domestic demand failed to expand fast enough to match rising output, and that this failure of demand to expand sufficiently was due to the inequality of income distribution. He preferred a solution based on greater equality of incomes. Failing this, so the argument runs, capitalists had to seek new investment ventures abroad in order to permit surplus capital to earn a good profit. Consequently, the owners of this surplus capital were supposed to exercise pressure on governments to acquire overseas territories, which would be reserved against investment by the nationals of other metropolitan powers.

This argument implies that all the colonial powers had surplus capital for which overseas outlets were required and also that the capital exported from each metropolitan power went, by and large, to its own colonial possessions. An examination of the empirical evidence shows, beyond any reasonable doubt, that neither proposition can be maintained. First, examination of the structures of business and commercial activities in the main European nations and the USA suggests that only in two cases, Germany and the USA, was there a sufficient concentration of financial control in a few hands to warrant the concept of 'finance capital' invented by Hilferding and dogmatically adopted by Bukharin and Lenin. Second, the substantial overseas investment that did occur in the nineteenth and early twentieth centuries was directed almost entirely to areas other than those acquired as colonies from c.1880 onwards; it went, instead, both to the industrializing countries and to nations such as Argentina, South Africa and Australia, where substantial European settlement had already taken place (Fieldhouse, 1973; Saul, 1960).

It would seem, therefore, on a cursory examination of the probabilities of the case, that the need for new openings for the profitable investment of capital made 'surplus' by the evolution of the European and North American economies is unlikely to have been the main cause of the expansion of formal colonization in the period after about 1870. (Fieldhouse, 1973, p. 61)

This conclusion is strongly reinforced if one examines the temporal evolution of *net* capital outflow from the industrializing nations. In the case of the United States, for example, it was only after the first world war that the volume of US investment abroad exceeded the flow of foreign investment into the country.

Britain was the single most important lender of capital throughout the nineteenth and early twentieth centuries, such that as late as 1914 'probably somewhere around half of the international investments belonged to the British and for much of the nineteenth century the proportion must have been a good deal higher' (Ashworth, 1975, p. 205). Clearly, the experience of this country deserves special attention. Some pertinent data are set out in Table 9 for the period 1816–1913. These data must be treated as estimates

Table 9 *United Kingdom balance of payments: net values, annual averages, 1816–1913*

Years	Merchandise trade	Overseas investment earnings	All other invisible trade	Bullion and specie	Over-all balance on current account*	Return on overseas lending (%)†
			£ million at current prices			
1816–9	−9.4	+1.5	+16.7	−0.7	+8.2	6.0
1820–9	−10.0	+4.3	+13.4	−1.0	+6.7	5.5
1830–9	−16.8	+6.4	+14.9	+0.3	+4.8	4.8
1840–9	−23.0	+8.3	+19.3	−0.5	+4.0	4.7
1850–9	−27.5	+13.2	+33.6	−3.5	+15.8	5.3
1860–9	−55.3	+24.6	+64.2	−4.3	+29.2	5.4
1870–4	−53.1	+45.5	+86.1	−5.3	+73.1	5.8
1875–9	−116.7	+56.4	+90.9	−2.4	+28.0	5.2
1880–4	−104.7	+62.2	+97.2	+1.3	+56.2	5.0
1885–9	−89.5	+79.4	+90.7	−0.4	+80.3	5.0
1890–4	−118.7	+94.1	+94.0	−5.8	+63.7	4.7
1895–9	−148.2	+98.2	+94.9	−4.7	+40.7	4.4
1900–4	−175.8	+109.0	+110.6	−3.6	+40.3	4.5
1905–9	−143.7	+142.1	+132.9	−2.6	+128.7	5.1
1910–13	−134.8	+183.5	+155.1	−7.3	+196.4	5.3

* Net lending abroad was of equal magnitude but opposite sign.
† The overseas investment earnings for a given year have been treated as the return on the 'accumulated credit abroad' as calculated by Imlah for the previous year.

Source: Imlah (1958), pp. 70–5.

Table 10   *Percentage real rate of profit on capital in British manufacturing industry, 1865–1909*

Years	Real rate of profit (%)
1865–9	16.5
1870–4	18.6
1875–9	15.2
1880–4	14.7
1885–9	15.0
1890–4	15.5
1895–9	15.2
1900–4	12.7
1905–9	11.9

Source: Cottrell (1980), p. 259.

that may be subject to substantial margins of error but nevertheless they are the best that are available. The column showing the over-all balance on current account can be treated as giving the magnitude of overseas lending. It was that flow of investment abroad which created the stock of assets which yielded the rising tide of overseas investment earnings evident in the second column. Whether, as Imlah (1958, p. 60) claims, the inflow of profits directly provided the funds for reinvestment abroad, or whether this investment had more general origins, is largely immaterial. Throughout the nineteenth century and early in the twentieth, Britain was a net lender. Furthermore, there was no sudden burst of additional investment after 1880, but rather a faltering thereof as a result of recession.

The final column of Table 9 indicates a rate of return on foreign investment at between 4 and 6 per cent. These figures are not independently derived but are based on estimates of the 'going' rate at various periods. That they are probably not too far from the mark is indicated by Lebergott's (1980) estimate that, in the period 1890–1929, the overseas investments of the United States raised the rate of return on US capital from just over 4.8 per cent to just under 4.9 per cent. If the data of Table 9 can be accepted as a fair approximation to the return on British overseas investment, comparison can be made with the return on capital in British manufacturing (Table 10). Although the rate of return fell between 1870–4 and 1905–9, it remained more than double the average profit on the whole portfolio of Britain's overseas investments. This fact, above all, confounds the proposition that the declining rate of profit at home drove capital to seek new outlets abroad. Thus, the sharp upswing in investment abroad as a proportion of total investment which occurred early in the present century (Table 11) should probably be regarded as an especially sharp upswing from a notably low trough rather than as evidence for a 'crisis' of capitalism. More generally, as Lewis (1978a, p. 143) remarks:

Economists have been expecting the rate of return on capital to decline ever since the middle of the eighteenth century, but this seems not to have happened.... One cannot be certain what happened to the rate of return of capital between 1870 and 1913, but allowing for ups and downs there is no reason to suspect a secular fall; most historians indeed have suspected a rise.

If this evidence appears to be surprising and counter-intuitive, confidence in its general veracity is reinforced when one considers the pattern of Britain's overseas investment in the period following the second world war (Table 12). The variation in average profitability, from 1.6 per cent in Argentina to 22.8 per cent in Germany, is striking. More significant is the lack of correlation between average profitability and the inflow of additional invest-

Table 11 *United Kingdom, overseas investment as a proportion of total investment, 1870–1913 (£ million at current prices)*

Years	Net domestic capital formation	Net lending abroad	Total net investment	Lending abroad as percentage of total
1870–4	81	65	146	45
1875–9	77	28	105	19
1880–4	96	63	159	40
1885–9	85	100	185	54
1890–4	84	78	162	48
1895–9	169	54	223	24
1900–4	174	46	220	21
1905–9	127	138	265	52
1910–13	128	202	230	61

Source: Ashworth (1960), p. 184.

Table 12 *Profitability of United Kingdom direct overseas investment, 1956–64*

Country	Post-tax profitability average 1956–64 (%)	Change in net operating assets, 1955–64, as percentage of assets in 1955
Germany	22.8	302
Malaysia	19.8	114
Ghana	13.4	−0.8
Italy	12.3	163
South Africa	10.5	44
USA	8.6	58
Jamaica	8.4	116
Australia	8.0	179
India	7.7	114
Canada	5.5	137
Denmark	5.3	218
Brazil	5.3	43
Nigeria	4.7	45
France	1.9	104
Argentina	1.6	137

Source: Reddaway, *et al.* (1968), p. 358.

ments. In the period covered by Table 12, it is evident that a multiplicity of considerations in addition to achieved profits must have been operative. It seems reasonable to suppose that a similar situation must have been evident in the period of frantic colonial expansion at the end of the nineteenth century.

The data examined above reinforce the conclusion reached by Fieldhouse, that economic considerations played a relatively small part in the acquisition of colonies. Whether his further conclusion is warranted is a matter that will need investigation:

The true 'capitalist imperialism' of Lenin's formula could and did operate primarily in his semi-colonies or commercial colonies generating the various types and degrees of informal empire that still existed in the second half of the twentieth century; and its really characteristic agent was the great international firm with subsidiaries throughout the non-socialist world rather than the capital-hungry colonizing adventurers typical of the age of expansive imperialism. (Fieldhouse, 1973, pp. 61–2)

An additional consideration, of great importance from the end of the nineteenth century until independence was achieved in the post-war period, is the manner in which the metropolitan powers organized their colonies. For if we accept, albeit tentatively, that the metropolitan powers did not gain economically so very much from their colonies, it is nevertheless possible that the colonies themselves experienced major impediments to development. The range of practice adopted by the major colonial powers was enormous, which renders generalization a hazardous business (for example, Royal Institute of International Affairs, 1937; Furnivall, 1948). Although the basic elements of infrastructure were established – transport and communications, education, etc. – the enterprise of indigenous peoples was often not fostered, or was even explicitly hindered. Even so, the reality cannot be expressed in simple, dogmatic terms, as is illustrated by the British East African Protectorate. While Leys (1975) argues the case for the adverse effects of British rule in Kenya, Wolff (1974) shows us the many faces of the development process. Acquired during the 'scramble for Africa' in the late nineteenth century, the Protectorate was perceived as impoverished and ill-organized compared with the circumstances in Uganda. One reason for this difference was the centuries-old tradition of slave trading along the East African coast. The British government took the view that colonies should, so far as possible, be financially self-sufficient. The colonial administration had to seek a quick way to raise the tax base and elected to foster the growing of export crops – maize, wheat, sisal and coffee were the early staples – with immigrant European farmers. Once a substantial immigrant community had been established, there was strong pressure for resources to be devoted to the 'white' areas and for the supply of cheap African labour to be maintained. This latter implied a low opportunity cost for African workers, which in turn implied little African development – indeed, the active discouragement thereof. While the effects were undoubtedly harmful to the medium-term development of the African peoples, this was not the initial intention and motivation but arose largely from the combination of time, place and the immigration of Europeans.

How permanent was the adverse impact of British rule in this part of Africa? Viewed from the perspective of 1981, it is striking how Uganda, which was never a colony, has squandered the advantages enjoyed until after the second world war. Tanzania, successor to Tanganyika and at one time under German rule, still struggles with her poverty. But Kenya is widely regarded as one of the most successful and prosperous of the newly independent African states.

The terms of trade

It is widely believed that the terms of trade between the more developed nations of the core and the less prosperous nations of the periphery have moved, and are continuing to move, in favour of the former and to the disadvantage of the latter. Thus, some will argue, the reality of colonial exploitation lives on even after nominal independence. There are two versions of this argument with which we will deal. The first is the 'theory of unequal exchange' which figures prominently in the Marxist and neo-Marxist literature, and which is readily shown to be fallacious. The second is the more orthodox problem of relative price movements over the medium to long term; in this case, the evidence is far from clear-cut one way or the other.

The 'theory' of unequal exchange, derived from the labour theory of value (p. 51), is dressed up in somewhat complicated language (for instance, Becker, 1977). Stripped of encumbrances, the proposition seems to be as follows. The production of goods involves the use of both 'constant' and 'variable' capital. The former is equivalent to the fixed costs associated with capital investment – the land, plant and machinery that comprise a factory. The latter is the materials used and the 'socially necessary labour' required for the production of goods; the greater part of this 'variable capital' is the labour component. If goods are exchanged at an equilibrating price which ensures the same rate of monetary profit on all commodities, then in the pre-capitalist era, i.e., at a time of relatively simple technology which is uniform among producers, the price of goods would be directly proportional to their value, which in turn would be proportional to the 'socially necessary labour' expended in their production. With technical development, production coefficients change unequally; relatively speaking, some lines of production become more capital intensive. It is easy to show that, for some goods where the 'constant capital' is large relative to the 'variable capital', the price received will be high in relation to the 'variable capital' used. By derivation, the price will be high relative to the 'socially necessary labour' *directly* expended in the production process; no account is taken of the labour represented by the 'constant capital'. Thus, the commodity price of the capital-intensive goods will be high relative to the man-hours of labour required, whereas the converse will be true of goods produced by relatively simple technology. The final step in the argument is to equate capital-intensive production with the core countries and labour-intensive activities with the periphery (Third World), and thereby to assert that 'unequal exchange' leads to the transfer of resources from the latter to the former.

It is on this basis that Amin (1973, p. 11), in the context of peasant groundnut producers, asserts that 'the "world market mechanism" is a synonym for robbery'. As he notes, the relative price of West African groundnuts on the world market was 'roughly stable from 1880 to 1968'. However, over this period productivity in France, the metropolitan country and main trading partner, rose steadily and rapidly, whereas little productivity improvement occurred in Senegal. As a consequence, the amount of (French) labour *directly* used to produce a basket of import goods in exchange for the groundnut output of a constant amount of Senegalese labour fell dramatically: the Senegalese peasant 'receives less than a seventh of what he received less than a century ago in terms of the value contained in the products exchanged' (Amin, 1973, p. 10).

The 'theory of unequal exchange' amounts only to the proposition that goods produced at a low level of productivity (i.e., generally with simple, traditional techniques) are likely to provide the workers with a lower standard of living than in the case where more advanced technology is employed. Therefore, the 'theory' is no theory at all. In the present context, the relevant question to ask is: why has productivity risen in some countries (or in some sectors) and not in others? To answer this question, a whole large field of investigation is opened up, which has nothing whatever to do with the labour theory of value.

Having shown that the 'theory of unequal exchange' is in fact specious, we must now turn our attention to the terms of trade considered more conventionally, a topic on which there is a very large literature. According to orthodox economic reasoning, agriculture and the other primary industries are subject to diminishing returns, whereas manufacturing enjoys increasing returns. Therefore, there ought to be a long-term tendency for the price of primary produce to rise relative to the price of manufactures. In practice, such a shift in the terms of trade in favour of primary producers does not seem to have occurred. Indeed, as Rostow (1978) notes, the currently received wisdom has fluctuated from fears of impending scarcity of foodstuffs and raw materials to the opposite anxiety, of

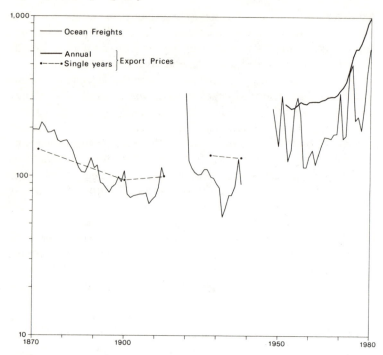

Figure 7   *Ocean freight rates and export prices, 1870–1980*
Sources: Kindleberger (1956), for the period 1870–1952 (these data refer to industrial European freight rates, and exports from industrial Europe); Chamber of Shipping of the United Kingdom, *Annual Reports*, for the period 1953–72 (these data refer to tramp time charter rates); United Nations, *Monthly Bulletin of Statistics*, for the period 1973–80 (these data refer to UK time charter dry cargo rates), and for the period 1953–80 (these data refer to world exports of manufactured goods).

a glut of primary produce and depressed prices thereof.

At face value, the comparison of import and export prices is relatively straightforward. In practice, there are many complications. Generalized import and export prices involve the familiar problems of index-number construction – availability and realiability of the raw data, choice of base year and the weighting system to be employed. In addition, there is the important distinction to be made between commodity comparisons and country comparisons. If commodities are classified into primary goods and manufactures, we cannot make direct inferences to provide a comparison between peripheral (developing) countries and the industrial nations of the core. While such inferences were valid for some countries in the nineteenth century, their general utility in the twentieth is questionable in the extreme. The matter is further complicated if, instead of the commodity terms of trade, one refers to the terms of trade on current account; this measure includes transactions such as shipping services. Merchandise terms of trade are generally constructed from export prices quoted f.o.b., whereas import prices are c.i.f. The latter, being the landed price at the point of import, include the costs of transport. Therefore, if transport costs fall, the c.i.f. value may drop without any change in the f.o.b. price in the country of origin. For the importer, the terms of trade (export price divided by import price) will improve but there will not be a symmetrical change for the exporter. Bairoch (1975, p. 117 ff.) argues cogently that over the period of 1876–80 to 1926–9, the reduction in transfer costs permitted the c.i.f. price of primary goods to fall about 12 per cent without any change in their f.o.b. value (Figure 7). This fact is sufficient to explain at least part of the lack of symmetry between changes in the terms of trade for Britain and India over the period 1861–1914 (Latham, 1978).

Bairoch also emphasizes the significance of the time period selected, arguing that many authors who cite evidence for a long-term and seemingly permanent shift in the terms of trade against primary manufactures have used data terminating in the depression years of the 1930s. The dangers are abundantly clear from Figure 8, which portrays the terms of trade for Britain from

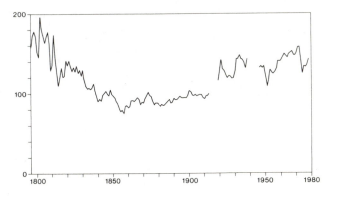

Figure 8   *British terms of trade, 1796–1978*
Sources: Mitchell and Deane (1971); *Annual Abstract of Statistics*.

1796 to 1978. Granted that a series spanning two centuries is subject to a considerable margin of error, it is apparent that in the early part of the modern era, until the 1850s, Britain's terms of trade deteriorated. The substantial recovery since then has been less rapid than the previous deterioration, has not brought the terms of trade back to the levels experienced early in the nineteenth century, and has been marked by some very severe fluctuations. During the 1950s and 1960s, there was widespread comment and complaint that the terms of trade were moving against primary producers and in favour of countries exporting manufactures. With the sharp increase in oil and commodity prices since 1973, these complaints have subsided, vindicating the view expressed by Kindleberger in 1964 that there was no necessity, either from theory or empirical evidence, why the then apparent trends must continue indefinitely.

That there has been a fairly sharp change in the terms of trade of major regions in recent years is shown by Table 13. Over the period 1960–77, the developed market economies have suffered from a deterioration of their commodity terms of trade. Japan, with her great reliance on imported materials and fuels, has been worst hit, but even South Africa, despite her rich mineral resources, has fared worse than the group as a whole. By contrast, the developing nations gained from a 50 per cent improvement in their terms of trade in the short period of 1970–7. Much of this improvement was due to the sharp increase in oil prices at the end of 1973 – hence the extraordinary improvement for the countries of the Asian Middle East. But Latin America and Africa also experienced a marked improvement (not just on account of oil-rich Venezuela and Nigeria) while Asia outside the Middle East has held its own. There is certainly nothing to suggest that in the period since 1960 the less developed countries have fared worse than the more advanced nations and indeed they have profited by changing relative prices.

Price changes are, however, only part of the story. An improvement in the commodity terms of trade implies that exports, being relatively dearer, may decline in volume. Conversely, imports may increase. Depending on the relevant elasticities, the gain from improved commodity terms of trade may be wiped out by differential changes in trade volume, or the loss from a worsening may be compensated by larger export volumes and fewer imports. To take account of this possibility, the double factoral terms of trade have been calculated for the period 1960–77 and are presented in Table 14. To derive these data, the following term has been used:

Table 13 *The commodity terms of trade for market economy countries, 1960–77 (1970 = 100)*

	1960	1965	1968	1969	1971	1972	1973	1974	1975	1976	1977
Developed market economies											
North America	96	98	99	99	99	100	99	87	90	89	89
Europe	96	98	101	101	98	95	96	88	89	89	85
South Africa	97	98	99	98	100	101	99	87	93	92	92
Israel and Japan	100	101	101	101	92	88	98	99	94	88	83
Australia and New Zealand	101	92	96	100	100	105	101	79	73	72	78
	109	113	101	102	93	103	134	108	90	88	100
Developing market economies											
Africa	103	99	100	101	103	103	114	156	140	146	151
Asia	104	97	102	106	101	102	114	154	128	142	146
Asian Middle East	109	99	102	100	107	104	110	171	155	161	162
Other Asia	116	109	109	104	117	115	124	311	275	280	276
Latin America	105	95	97	99	97	96	101	94	86	94	101
	94	100	96	97	100	100	113	126	119	119	131

Source: United Nations *Statistical Yearbook, 1978* (1979), p. 54.

$$\frac{E_p}{I_p} \times \frac{E_q}{I_q} \times 100$$

where E_p is the export price index, I_p is the import price index, and E_q and I_q are respectively the index values for export quantity and import quantity. In effect, the commodity terms of trade E_p/I_p is multiplied by the ratio of export and import volumes.

Comparison of Tables 13 and 14 shows very clearly how changes in the volume of exports and imports modify the picture presented by changes in the commodity terms of trade. In one case, that of North America, the adverse effects of deteriorating commodity terms of trade are amplified by a high growth rate of imports relative to exports; for all the other groups of developed economies identified, trade changes more than offset the deterioration in the terms of trade. This effect has been particularly beneficial for Japan. Over the period 1960–77, the terms of trade moved in favour of the developing countries, and particularly the oil-exporting nations from 1974 onwards. Part of the benefit to the developing nations, and especially the oil exporters, has been offset by sluggish trade in their export staples and rapid increase in imports. Nevertheless, with the exception of Latin America – which has registered only a small net gain – Table 14 shows that all the other groups of developing countries have benefited substantially from the combined effects of price and quantum changes.

Dependence and underdevelopment

There is a school of thought which holds that underdevelopment is a modern phenomenon, created by the impact of the more advanced economies on the archaic structures of nations in the world's periphery (Furtado, 1964). Thus, whereas in the 1950s it was widely held that underdevelopment was a stage through which the developed nations had passed, it was now postulated that the underdeveloped nations are a new category, a response to the impact of capitalist development (Frank, 1966 and 1967; dos Santos, 1970; Brewer, 1980). Several strands may be detected in this school of thought, though not all are necessarily held by all the individual authors. However, a common theme is that countries in the Third World are not able to control their destinies, being dependent in numerous ways on one or more of the core nations and suffering thereby.

Table 14 *The double factoral commodity terms of trade for market economy countries, 1960–77 (1970 = 100)*

	1960	1965	1968	1969	1971	1972	1973	1974	1975	1976	1977
Developed market economies	100	98	99	100	100	101	100	94	100	96	97
North America	111	105	95	95	90	84	94	87	95	85	78
Europe	99	96	101	101	102	104	102	98	102	100	101
South Africa	131	100	135	119	89	122	121	102	101	110	175
Israel and Japan	86	100	97	104	119	117	95	87	95	102	112
Australia and New Zealand	86	89	91	102	105	130	134	89	105	108	102
Developing market economies	91	98	98	100	100	106	118	143	115	126	119
Africa	69	84	97	107	87	98	104	124	81	97	89
Asia	95	95	98	98	112	117	125	171	134	152	138
Asian Middle East	87	95	99	98	120	114	122	205	142	134	112
Other Asia	101	95	95	99	102	115	122	115	107	128	130
Latin America	94	116	95	88	93	96	105	100	90	97	101

Source: United Nations *Statistical Yearbook, 1978*, pp. 52–4.

First, the allegedly dominant 'capitalist' mode of production has ensured an 'outward directed' pattern of development in the peripheral nations, especially Latin America and Africa, geared to supply the needs of the core nations, especially for foodstuffs and raw materials. This highly selective 'development', it is argued, has very limited multiplier effects and therefore stimulates negligible further growth. Meantime, indigenous enterprise is seriously damaged, even destroyed, by the impact of manufactured imports. By a variety of means, including the operations of multinational companies, it is alleged that a net transfer of resources is taking place from the poor nations to the rich. All of this is said to be underpinned by the technological dominance of the advanced economies, such that their advantages are reinforced by the *kind* of new technological advances, which are suited to the conditions of the rich but not the poor nations (Singer and Ansari, 1977).

In the space available it is impossible to examine all of these contentions in detail. Indeed, the translation of many of them into testable hypotheses presents formidable problems, as witness the valiant but only partially successful efforts of Mahler (1980). We will concentrate our attention on just one of the contentions, one which appears to be fundamental to a good deal of the dependency theorizing. It is postulated that there is a net transfer of resources from the poor nations to the rich; whether these resources are called profits, capital or surplus value is relatively unimportant. Nor is it fundamental to the argument whether the mechanism be the operation of multinational companies, manipulation of the terms of trade or other means.

Frank (1964, p. 295) has roundly condemned the main industrial countries in the following terms: 'The developing metropolitan powers pillaged the peoples in these political and economic colonies of capital which they used to industrialize their own economies.' Elsewhere, he elaborates a concept of hierarchical spatial organization in which there is a net transfer of resources *upwards*, from the rural areas of underdeveloped nations to the regional capitals, thence to the national capitals and onwards to the capitals of the major metropolitan powers, for example, London, New York and Paris. Frank cites Latin American evidence in support of this contention but the evidence is in fact tendentiously inadequate. In the case of Brazil, he compares the inflow from the USA of investment funds on private account with the reverse flow of funds. The latter includes profits, royalties, interest, etc. and is pretty comprehensive in its scope. The former, the inflow of funds, is partial in its coverage, since it excludes investment and loans by government and international agencies. Similarly misleading comparisons have been made by Jørgensen (1979) for Uganda in the period 1966–70.

Available evidence does not support the contention of Frank and others that there is a net transfer of funds from the poorer to the richer countries. Contemporary balance of payments data are collected and published by the International Monetary Fund; summary data are contained in the *Statistical Yearbook* issued by the United Nations. These tabulations itemize trade in merchandise and services, which we will leave to one side, plus capital and other forms of transaction. These include private and government unrequited transfers net, direct investment, other long-term capital transfers, short-term capital movements, the monetization of gold, and changes in reserves and related items. The aggregate of these non-trade transactions includes the movements of capital for investment, loans and repatriated profits. If the dependency school of thought is correct in its assertion that net transfers of resources are occurring from the periphery to the core nations, then the aggregate balance on the non-trade headings should be negative for a least a substantial number of the poorer, less developed nations. Were this to be the case, the maintenance of equilibrium in the international balance of payments would require that these countries earn a surplus on trade in merchandise and services.

The 1980 issue of the United Nations *Statistical Yearbook* gives information for 112 countries (outside the COMECON group), mostly for 1977 but in some cases for an earlier year if more recent information is not available. Of the 112 nations, only twenty-three experienced a net outflow of funds under the non-trade headings. These twenty-three countries fall into three groups, as:

Developed	*Developing*	
	Oil-rich	*Other*
Belgium	Iran	Argentina
West Germany	Iraq	Bahamas
Italy	Kuwait	Colombia
Japan	Libya	Equatorial Guinea
Netherlands	Saudi Arabia	Gabon
South Africa		Netherlands Antilles
Switzerland		Sri Lanka
United Kingdom		Swaziland
United States		Uganda

With the major exceptions of Canada, France, Sweden and Australia, the majority of the world's developed countries outside the COMECON bloc experienced a net transfer of funds abroad – trade balances excluded. Major oil-producing states were also important sources for monetary transfers abroad. Only nine countries fit the model proposed by the dependency theorists, i.e., poor developing states experiencing a net transfer of funds abroad. This is a very small proportion of the world's developing nations. With the exception of Argentina, Sri Lanka and Uganda, the nine states listed above are of minor economic importance. More significant is the fact that special circumstances can be adduced in at least some cases to account for the net outflow of resources under the non-trade headings. Perhaps the most obvious instance is Uganda, where the regime of President Amin created a climate of such fear and uncertainty that disinvestment had been proceeding for some years prior to 1977.

Table 15 presents a selection of aggregate data for 1978, being the net credits and debits of the industrial nations and the developing countries collectively under a number of headings. The broad

Table 15   *Summary of international transactions, 1978 (thousand million SDRs*)*

	Industrial countries		Developing countries	
	Credit	Debit	Credit	Debit
Merchandise f.o.b.	627.0	615.0	203.2	181.9
Other goods, services and income	233.7	211.2	48.6	84.0
Private unrequited transfers	6.5	12.5	7.8	3.9
Official unrequired transfers	10.8	26.9	5.4	4.4
Direct investment	—	13.8	5.7	—
Portfolio investment	6.1	—	1.2	—
Other long-term capital	—	13.8	19.9	—
Other short-term capital	19.5	—	—	6.2
Net errors and omissions	19.2	—	0.2	—
Reserves	—	29.3	—	11.4

* SDRs are units of account which have a variable relationship to the United States dollar; 1 SDR≏US$ 1.

Source: International Monetary Fund, supplement to *Balance of Payments Yearbook*, vol. 30 (1979), p. 40.

pattern is immediately evident. The industrial countries earned an over-all surplus on trade in goods and services, which was offset by net deficits under most of the other headings. For the developing countries, the pattern was reversed. Over all, there is no evidence to suggest a net drain of resources from the poorer to the richer nations. At the aggregate level for all the developing countries, the reinvestment of earnings on direct investment, plus all other investment income, contributed 11 billion SDRs credit and 26.5 billion debit to the respective totals of 48.6 billion and 84 billion shown in Table 15 for 'other goods, services and income'. Thus, although there is a net flow of investment income out of the developing countries, this is fully compensated by other transfers. This conclusion is not disturbed when the developing countries are grouped into the oil-exporting nations, other western hemisphere developing countries, and the developing nations of the Middle East, Asia and Africa; the same general pattern is observable for all the groups except the oil-rich developing countries, which in fact have a surplus of funds available for investment abroad.

Trade as an 'engine of growth'

Borrowing the term from Robertson, Nurkse (1962) regarded the expansion of international trade as an 'engine of growth' throughout much of the nineteenth century. Part of the consequential develop- ment would be a once-and-for-ever gain arising from the realization of comparative advantage as transport cost and other impediments to commerce were reduced. In addition: 'As I see it, it was also a means whereby a vigorous process of economic growth came to be transmitted from the center to the outlying areas of the world (Nurkse, 1962, p. 14).' According to this view, the rising population of the core countries, increasing industrialization and improving standards of living created growing demands for foodstuffs and raw materials from abroad. The export of these products thus paved the way for a process of continuous further growth in countries of the periphery.

Trade, whether interregional or international, occurs in response to comparative cost differences which are not fully offset by transfer costs. These cost differences arise from a number of sources. Classical economists identified comparative advantage in terms of resource endowments, whereas Heckscher and Ohlin formulated a more general statement in terms of factor proportions. Both of these versions of trade theory are essentially 'static', in the sense that as trade barriers (transport costs, tariffs, etc.) are removed, a reallocation of production occurs to the mutual benefit of the parties involved. In addition, long-term dynamic effects can be expected if there are economies of scale in production; trade expansion will permit a reduction in unit costs. There will also be trade gains of a dynamic nature arising from technological changes. With the steady development of new products and new ways of making old goods, the number of available production functions may be substantial. As technology diffuses, international trade arises from cost advantages which are, at least in part, man made (Hufbauer, 1966).

During the nineteenth century and early in the twentieth, the main benefits of trade arose from a combination of the 'static' effects identified above and the rising level of demand in the core countries. Technical developments in transport and communications in the nineteenth century facilitated very rapid expansion of international trade. As Latham (1978) points out, it was not just a matter of steam ships replacing sail and the expansion of railway networks across the major land masses. In addition, the opening of the Suez Canal in 1869 and the Panama Canal in 1914 reduced the distance of many ocean routes dramatically. A matching development was that of the telegraph, which made possible the world-wide transmission of information about commodity needs, supplies, prices and shipments, information which was essential if international commerce were to be conducted on an efficient basis. Not until 1886, when a cable along the west coast of Africa was laid, did the basic skeleton of international telegraph links become reasonably complete. Associated with these and other developments, the cost of international freight transport fell dramatically, as shown in Figure 7 (p. 72).

Despite the rapidity of these technical advances and the growth of manufacturing in Britain and Western Europe, it was only in the last quarter of the nineteenth century that trade became a *world-wide* engine of growth for peripheral nations, and even then the beneficial effects were felt very selectively (Cairncross, 1962; Lewis, 1978a). Table 16 summarizes what are admittedly rather tentative estimates of the growth of world trade and industrial production. Until 1913, world trade grew at a pace roughly to match the tempo of industrial growth; in the period 1840–70, trade expanded especially quickly. Between 1913 and 1948, with the world wars and serious recession in the 1930s, trade grew very sluggishly indeed. Subsequently, the growth of industrial output and of trade has been very rapid.

Table 16 *World trade and industrial production, annual average percentage growth, 1720–1977*

Years	World trade	World industrial production
1720–80	1.10	1.5*
1780–1830	1.37	2.6
1820–40	2.81	2.9
1840–60	4.84	3.5
1860–70	5.53	2.9
1870–1900	3.24	3.7
1900–13	3.75	4.2
1913–29	0.72	2.7
1929–38	−1.15	2.0
1938–48	0.00	4.1
1948–71	7.27	5.6
1971–7	5.30	6.1

* 1707–85.

Sources: Rostow (1978), p. 67; United Nations *Statistical Yearbook, 1978*, pp. 25 and 52–3.

The period to which Nurkse referred was the first of these three, and initially we will also confine our attention to the same span of years, in which the engine of growth actually only affected part of the world's periphery. To understand why this was so, it is useful to review briefly some basic ideas in location theory.

Figure 9 depicts the basic relationships of the von Thünen model of agricultural location as originally published in 1826. (See Chisholm, 1979, for a summary, and Hall, 1966, for a translation of von Thünen's major work.) Abstracting from variations in the physical environment, and also spatially differentiated costs of production and transport, one can readily visualize that in response to the relative tonnage of output per hectare and the consequential costs of transport, zones of production around the consumption centre will become established. In Figure 9, potatoes will be grown between O and Y, and wheat at greater distances. Whereas von Thünen conceived of his market centre as a single city, Schlebecker (1960) and Chisholm (1979) point out that on a global scale the major metropolitan area, or indeed the core nations, may be regarded the market around which production zones will develop.

With the long-term growth of population in the core nations, and rising incomes, the demand for foodstuffs has increased. If transport improvements were the only technical change to occur, the revenue curves AB and CD in Figure 9 would become flatter and supplies could be drawn from further afield; the zones of production would expand outward. However, with technical changes in production, yields have in fact been increasing over at least the last one and a half centuries. In practice, therefore, higher domestic production in the core, and especially Western Europe, has met a substantial part of the increased food needs and large-scale imports only became necessary after the middle of the nineteenth century.

Towards the end of the century, rising incomes began to be expressed in terms of a proportionately greater demand for meat, liquid milk, fruit and vegetables. Grain was now readily available from distant lands, and from the 1880s onwards the application of refrigeration to sea-going vessels meant that meat and dairy produce could be shipped half way round the world and yet remain in good condition.

Two papers by Peet (1969 and 1972) examine the impact of expanding European, and especially British, demand for temperate

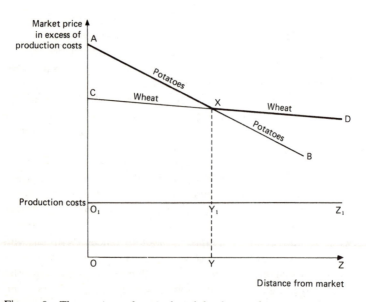

Figure 9 *The zoning of agricultural land use about a market centre: revenues for production from one hectare, assuming no cost for land*

agricultural products. Initially, the expansion of supply zones affected mainland Europe itself, rather than more distant lands – especially the North Sea coastlands of Holland, Germany and Denmark, and lands such as Poland and Western Russia accessible to the Baltic. However, only some regions were able to respond to the challenge presented by rising urban demand. Denmark, Prussia and Poland in particular, and to some extent Hungary and Russia, were able to expand their output of either grain or livestock, or both. Only those countries which were able to make the transition to livestock, and especially dairy produce and pigmeat products, subsequently maintained their position as exporters. The facility or otherwise with which this transition was made appears to have depended very much upon the differing structure of the farming sector; independent peasant farmers responded better than the large landed estates (Warriner, 1939).

As the nineteenth century wore on, the opening of temperate lands for European colonization with grain and livestock products among the major initial export staples, provided the basis for very rapid economic expansion in a number of peripheral countries. By comparison, the impact on the densely populated tropical nations was much less evident. Several reasons may be offered to explain why this was so. Where the tropical countries were competing with products from temperate latitudes (about half their total exports), a high level of commercial efficiency was necessary; this proved hard to achieve and its want militated against expansion of exports in this range of products. In addition, the period of buoyant demand for products peculiar to the tropics came somewhat later than for temperate produce, reflecting the changing pattern of industrial production and consumer preferences. Finally, the absolute size of the population in Asia, Africa and Latin America meant that however strong the impulse for development may have been, its impact on the tropical nations was in general of much less significance proportionally than in the case of the sparsely inhabited countries of European settlement. In sum, for the tropics in the period 1880–1913, trade provided the stimulus which led to the laying of the foundations for subsequent growth, rather than to evident and sustained growth during that period (Lewis, 1970). But, just as the response within Europe varied considerably, so the pattern within the tropical world showed great divergence.

If we turn our attention to minerals, fuels and vegetable products for manufacturing, an analysis analogous to that used in Figure 9

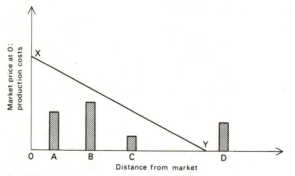

Figure 10   *Market price, transport costs and production costs for a mineral at various sites*

can be employed. Imagine four sites at which a given material can be produced, with the unit production costs represented by the height of the columns at A, B, C and D (Figure 10). Given the market price at O, and transport costs, the price that will be received at any location is indicated by the line XY. Other things being equal, site A would be exploited first, since the difference between unit cost and unit price is here the greatest. With the exhaustion of A, C would next be used and then B. In the absence of an increase in market price and therefore upward movement of XY, or a diminution in transport costs and flattening of the XY curve, site D would remain uneconomic and therefore unused.

In the case of minerals, the cost of production is affected by the depth of the deposit and its quality. Therefore, interpreting Figure 10 one should have in mind that the spatial dimension is not the only one to be considered. Nevertheless, other things being equal, those deposits which are located nearest to the centres of demand will be exploited before those which are further away. With the advance of industrialization in Britain and Europe during the nineteenth century, most of the requisite raw materials lay close to hand – coal, iron ore and non-ferrous metals such as copper and tin. With the major exception of textile materials and timber, Britain and her continental rivals were largely self-sufficient in fuels and materials until after 1850. Partly because deposits were exhausted, and partly because, short of exhaustion, they ceased to be economic to work, imports became increasingly necessary. Where possible, these imports were drawn from nearby sources rather than from far afield. Towards the end of the century, these relatively local supplies

proved inadequate. Furthermore, as technological change acceler-
ated, the need arose for materials that are not available in Europe,
or are available in inadequate amounts, such as bauxite and
vegetable oils (Lewis, 1978a).

In this context, we should also note that the techniques of
reconnaissance geological survey awaited the advent of aircraft and
the development of geophysics. As a consequence, until after the
second world war, the discovery of mineral deposits depended in
substantial measure on chance. Until well into the twentieth century
there was a much higher probability of minerals being discovered
and exploited in the regions of European settlement than elsewhere,
although there were notable exceptions, such as tin mining in
Malaya.

In the light of the foregoing discussion, it is readily apparent why
Sweden was a potential beneficiary of the industrial expansion that
occurred in Britain, Germany and France. The modern economic
era was initiated by the timber industry: 'It was this industry, far
more than any other, which transformed the economic life of
Sweden from about the 1850s' (Youngson, 1959, p. 112). Timber
had been the only bulk trade of the eighteenth century, with Britain
as one of the major markets. However, this trade declined sharply
early in the nineteenth century. With the independence of America,
achieved in 1776, Britain's main supply of ships' masts was put at
peril. Subsequently, during the Napoleonic Wars, all continental
timber supplies for ship construction were in jeopardy, and Britain
turned to Canada. In response to high prices and the then substantial
bounties and preferences, Canada became the main Imperial source
of timber, and Scandinavia was neglected. With the ending of
preferences of any significance in 1851, the Baltic region could
resume its position as Britain's main supplier (Lower, 1973).

For a variety of reasons, it was Sweden that was able to rise to the
challenge in a spectacular fashion. In effect, there was a sudden and
major impulse to development generated by the removal of trade
barriers, so that relatively proximate sources of supply could be
exploited on a large scale. As Youngson (1959) notes, this development implied a major programme of investment in ports, etc., and
also fundamental changes in the production techniques and in
timber extraction and processing – changes which paved the way for
future development. Viewed on a global scale, the industrial
expansion and associated material demands of Britain in particular,
and other European countries, provided a major impulse for

development in nearby nations, of which Sweden was the one to respond most dramatically.

Trade as an engine of growth during the last part of the nineteenth century and up to the first world war was an apt description for some countries. It appears to be true of Denmark and Sweden, but not of Eastern Europe, which could have supplied foodstuffs, timber and minerals, but failed to rise to the challenge, probably for institutional reasons associated with land tenure and the structure of society. The trade impetus to growth was also immensely important for Argentina and Uruguay in Latin America, South Africa and Zimbabwe (formerly Southern Rhodesia) in Africa, Australia and New Zealand, and, to a lesser extent, in Sri Lanka (formerly Ceylon). Elsewhere, there was a significant impact, but this was inadequate to get sustained development going, for example, on the west coast of Africa. For countries such as India, Pakistan, Bangladesh, Iraq and Iran, the export trades were too small relative to the total population to provide much impetus to development, except in very restricted areas. As for oil, Venezuela and Mexico were two of the countries which were early beneficiaries but it was not until the Middle East became a major supplier after the second world war that the trade engine of growth really applied to Saudi Arabia, the Gulf States, and then subsequently to Libya and Algeria. But by this time, the engine was faltering elsewhere.

As Cairncross (1962) points out, international trade permits a once-for-all increase in wealth on account of specialization of production on the basis of relative advantages of soil, climate and natural endowment generally. However, this does not necessarily indicate a sustained process of further growth and development. It is now quite clear that it was much easier for this to occur in some European countries, and in countries of European settlement, than in those societies where a transformation of economic and social relationships would be required (see Chapter 5). Viewed in the long-term perspective, two distinct mechanisms can be identified in this context. The plantation economies of Sri Lanka, Indonesia and elsewhere may provide an improved standard of living for those directly employed, but the general impact on development is indirect, through the generation of revenues for use by government. Mineral exploitation is directly analogous. In both cases, the initial and potentially long-enduring pattern is that of the so-called 'dual economy', with enclaves of export-oriented development set in a matrix of little change. By contrast, exports by peasant producers yield widely dispersed profits which, over a period of time, lay the basis for a widespread, even if slow, rise in purchasing power of the population at large. This in turn will make possible a fundamental change in attitudes which ultimately ought to provide a sound basis for long-term development. Necessarily, however, this cannot be expected to yield spectacular results; the relevant time span will be decades at the very least. Hopkins (1973) argues that this is the true significance of peasant production of palm oil, groundnuts and cacao in West Africa, while a similar argument applies to the peasant production of rubber in Malaya and rice for export from Lower Burma.

The periphery industrializes

The colonial powers had no particular incentive to foster industrialization in their overseas possessions. Such industrialization was regarded in influential quarters as a threat to established businesses in the metropolitan states, and was therefore in many cases actively discouraged. For example, the British in India followed policies which discriminated against Indian entrepreneurs in a manner that seems to have been prejudicial to development (Bagchi, 1972), although in the case of steel a more realistic assessment is probably that policy was based on compromise between the needs of British and Indian manufacturers (Wagle, 1981).

During the first world war and then again during the second world conflict, international trade patterns were seriously disrupted. Independent nations, especially those in Latin America (Mexico, Brazil and Argentina most especially) found that they had an opportunity to develop manufacturing industries to replace imports that either were not available or else were scarce. India also was able to profit from this situation. For the majority of colonial territories, the more important events were probably the recession which started in 1929 and the new international political alignment which emerged after the second world war. In response to the inter-war slump, the major industrial nations sought to protect their own interests by trade restrictions and protectionist policies generally. Primary producing countries were particularly hard hit by the drop in demand and the associated reduction in prices of their export commodities. Under the circumstances, it was difficult for the metropolitan powers to deny the right of dependencies to follow policies designed to bolster their economies, with industrial development an obvious strategy. Before anything very tangible could occur, rearmament began, the recession abated and war broke out in 1939. Nevertheless, important changes of attitude had occurred which paved the way for a fundamental, almost revolutionary, transformation after the war.

Within about a decade of the cessation of hostilities, the majority of major colonial countries in Africa and Asia had achieved independence or were on the threshold thereof. The newly independent nations were eager to foster their own development, the core nations were generally sympathetic to this aspiration, and experience with the reconstruction of Europe's economy under the Marshall Plan suggested that radical changes could be wrought quickly. Furthermore, the rivalry of America and Russia ensured the flow of resources from both superpowers to assist the development of putatively friendly states all over the world; Mackinder's concept of the pivot of power in Asia and the girdle of encircling areas had an immediacy of application that was visible to both the major powers and the lesser ones as well (Mabogunje, 1980a). Finally, a whole series of international trade agreements has served to reduce, though not to eliminate, impediments to the world-wide movement of goods, while permitting Third World countries to protect their own infant industries. From the convergence of these and other streams of thought and action, the post-war decades have witnessed a remarkable drive to industrialize in countries of the periphery, a drive which has had much more support from the core countries than might have been expected. A major reason for this relatively high level of cooperation has been the phenomenal rate of growth that characterized the major industrial states up to the early 1970s. With faltering growth/recession since 1973, and deep recession in 1980–1, the pressure on governments in the more advanced nations to impose import restrictions and limit overseas aid has been growing greater and therefore the continued cooperation of the core countries cannot be taken for granted (Table 17).

In principle, three forms of industrialization are available to countries with initially a negligible industrial sector. The pattern will vary according to local circumstances, primarily the natural resource endowment and the size of the population. The export of primary materials invites local processing in order to raise the value added prior to shipment, and hence the aggregate benefit to the exporting country. Such processing usually increases the unit value of the export commodity and thereby reduces the inhibiting effects of

Table 17 *World production, percentage annual growth 1961–79 (in 1977 prices)*

	1961–73	1974–9
Gross domestic product		
World	5.4	3.6
Developed market economies	5.0	2.7
Developing countries	6.0	5.2
Oil-exporting	7.5	5.4
Non-oil-exporting	5.4	5.2
Centrally planned economies	6.7	5.2
Industrial production		
World	6.8	3.5
Developed market economies	5.6	2.2
Developing countries	7.3	3.9
Centrally planned economies	8.1	6.3

Source: United Nations, *World Economic Survey 1979–1980: Current Trends in the World Economy* (1980), p. 14.

transport costs. However, this form of industrialization can be seriously limited by the structure of tariffs on imports into the core nations. A very common pattern is for unprocessed raw materials to be admitted without tariff or other restriction but for high and perhaps insurmountable obstacles to be placed in the way of processed materials. In practice, some compromise has been reached, though there seems little doubt that the rate of export processing industrialization has been limited by tariffs and other import controls. Despite difficulties of this kind, the Philippines has successfully transformed her export of logs into trade in sawn timber, plywood and similar products. Much of Bangladesh's jute is now processed before export, and Argentina has for many years exported canned meat in addition to frozen carcases.

The scope for industrialization along the above lines is limited and from such a base it is most unlikely that a diverse pattern of manufacturing could emerge, as New Zealand has found. Thus, the second strategy is import substitution. Basic consumer commodities, such as beer and soft drinks, bicycles and electric light bulbs, clothing and furniture, are all of a kind that can be made with reasonably straightforward technology. Their local manufacture or assembly will create employment and save foreign exchange (once the necessary capital investment has been completed). It may be possible to sell the finished articles more cheaply than the equivalent imported goods, but this is not usually the case in the initial years. A widespread problem is that the initial scale of output may be small and, while the workforce is gaining experience, productivity may be low; consequently, unit costs are apt to be high.

To compensate for these disadvantages, the infant industry argument justifies protection during the early years, usually in the form of duties on imports. In theory, once the industry is established, the protection will be reduced and ultimately removed. There is the substantial risk that the protected industries will be inefficient and fail to achieve competitiveness, and that vested interests will ensure the continuation of assistance more or less indefinitely. Probably the most careful study of protection as it has been practised is that carried out by Balassa and his colleagues (1971); some of their summary data are shown in Table 18. The nominal protection afforded to industry is the level of import duty levied. To convert this nominal protection to net protection, three adjustments have been made. The first is to take account of the protection afforded

Table 18   *Industrial protection, selected developing countries in the 1960s*

Country*	Net effective protection, manufacturing (%) D‡	F§	The 'cost' of protection, percentage of GNP	Manufacturing exports as percentage of total exports† c. 1950	c. 1967
Brazil (1966)	68	79	9.5	0.7	9.9
Chile (1961)	68	54	6.2	(3)	4.7
Mexico (1960)	16	21	2.5	8.7	21.1
Malaya (1965)	−10	7	−0.4	(1)	7.8
Pakistan (1963–4)	147	92	6.2	(1)	43.2
Philippines (1965)	41	34	3.7	3.7	9.9

* Dates refer to the first three columns.
† Figures in parentheses are based on an incomplete commodity breakdown.
‡ D = estimates based on domestic input–output coefficients.
§ F = estimates based on free-trade input–output coefficients.

Source: Balassa, *et al.* (1971), pp. 45, 56 and 82.

to the inputs of a manufacturing industry – components, part-manufacturers, etc. Next, the effective protection can be calculated as the value added in manufacture in the particular country compared with a 'world' (free market) level of value added. The final adjustment is to calculate the value added ratio if there were no foreign exchange restraints on the currency.

For the sample of countries, the general level of protection is high, with the notable exception of Malaya. Balassa, who is a confirmed free-trader by inclination, estimates that the static 'cost' of protection is a significant proportion of gross national product for all the countries except Malaya. On the whole, Balassa took the view that protection tends to make countries poorer than they otherwise would be. This rather pessimistic view is at least partially belied by the data in Table 18 for the proportion that manufactures are of total exports. With the exception of Chile and the Philippines, manufactures accounted for a much larger proportion of exports in 1967 than in 1950, though the figures for Pakistan – prior to the formation of Bangladesh – are misleading in that almost all the 'manufactures' were processed fibres.

When examined on an industry-by-industry basis, Balassa's data show the kind of pattern that is expected. Consumer goods enjoyed the highest levels of protection, primary goods the lowest; protection was generally greatest for the most highly fabricated goods. In extreme cases, net effective protection exceeded 400 per cent (certain food products in Brazil). Sixty-seven commodities were examined for the six countries, making a matrix with 402 cells. Altogether, thirty-one of the cells, or nearly 8 per cent of the observations, registered protection at over 100 per cent.

Apart from the potential problems of high-cost, inefficient production, import substitution industrialization suffers from one major limitation – the small absolute size of the available market, even in populous countries. The smallness of the market is due to the high proportion of the population engaged in agriculture, the low productivity of labour in this sector and hence low effective demand. Some of the early starters were reaching the limits to import substitution industrialization by the end of the 1960s.

Lewis (1978b) briefly but cogently argues that the period since 1960 has witnessed a major change in the structure of the world economy. Whether measured in terms of volume or of value, the growth of manufactured imports from the less developed nations has been phenomenal. As Table 19 shows, whereas the industrial

Table 19 World exports of primary products, manufactures and total by areas, 1963–76, volume indices (1970 = 100)

Origin / Destination	Year	Industrial areas Primary products	Manufactures	Total	Developing areas Primary products	Manufactures	Total	World* Primary products	Manufactures	Total
Value ($ thou. million)	1970	37.7	121	161	6.4	31.7	39.7	46.2	165	216
	1963	64	45	50	66	61	62	65	49	53
	1968	86	81	82	88	82	81	86	81	82
	1970	100	100	100	100	100	100	100	100	100
Industrial areas	1971	101	108	106	105	106	106	102	107	106
	1972	111	122	119	105	109	108	111	118	116
	1973	123	136	132	127	124	124	126	134	132
	1974	123	143	138	129	156	149	125	147	142
	1975	117	129	126	132	170	163	120	140	136
	1976	130	148	143	—	183	—	131	157	151
Value ($ thou. million)	1970	30.5	9.3	40.5	7.3	3.7	11.0	42.1	13.8	56.0
	1963	65	46	61	75	48	66	67	46	61
	1968	88	73	83	94	66	84	88	71	82
	1970	100	100	100	100	100	100	100	100	100
Developing areas	1971	106	106	106	99	103	104	103	105	104
	1972	113	124	117	115	130	123	112	125	116

Table 19 continued

The periphery industrializes 95

Origin / Year	Industrial areas			Developing areas			World*		
	Primary products	Manufactures	Total	Primary products	Manufactures	Total	Primary products	Manufactures	Total
Developing areas									
1973	123	154	130	130	148	139	122	151	130
1974	115	158	124	131	179	149	118	164	128
1975	103	151	114	134	206	162	111	166	124
1976	116	194	134	—	234	—	—	203	—
Value ($ thou. million)									
1970	76.5	134	214	15.6	39.1	57.4	103	203	312
1963	65	46	53	70	59	62	68	50	56
1968	88	80	83	92	81	82	88	81	83
1970	100	100	100	100	100	100	100	100	100
World*									
1971	103	108	106	104	105	105	103	107	106
1972	113	121	118	111	110	110	112	118	116
1973	125	137	133	127	125	126	124	134	130
1974	119	145	135	131	155	147	119	146	137
1975	111	131	123	137	169	159	115	141	132
1976	123	152	142	—	184	—	—	158	(148)

* Including the Eastern bloc trading area, Australia, New Zealand and South Africa.

Source: GATT (1978), Table D.1.

nations of the world increased their export volume of manufactures by a factor of just over three between 1963 and 1976, the developing areas achieved growth by a factor of over four in the same period. Furthermore, the developing areas were almost as successful in the expansion of industrial exports to the industrial nations as to other developing countries and in absolute volume the industrial nations have been much more important customers than the rest of the world. Perhaps the other key feature of Table 19 is the growth of primary exports from the developing nations at a much slower tempo than the expansion of manufactured exports. The developing areas failed to expand their export of primary goods to the industrial nations at a pace to match the growth of intra-industrial trade in primary commodities. On the other hand, their exports of manufactures to the industrial nations rose faster than the intra-industrial trade in manufactured goods, which was a very substantial achievement.

The trade flows summarized in Table 19 can be examined in much more detail in terms of values than quantities, although value data must be treated with caution because of the impact of differential price movements, which have been substantial during the last two decades. GATT distinguishes the oil-exporting countries from the other developing nations, but only from 1970. Between 1955 and 1970, manufactured exports from all developing areas rose from $3.05 thousand million to $13.90 thousand million at current prices. In the comparable period, world exports of manufactures increased in value from $45.35 thousand million to $202.65 thousand million, also at current prices. Between 1970 and 1975, world trade in manufactures expanded to $519.30 thousand million. By contrast, the oil-exporting developing countries achieved a very modest growth, from $0.45 thousand million in 1970 to $1.40 thousand million in 1975, whereas the other developing countries advanced from $13.45 thousand million to $35.70 thousand million. Provisional figures for 1976 show a spectacular jump of $11.80 thousand million to a total of $47.50 thousand million, compared with a world-wide increase to $588.80 thousand million. Of the $47.50 thousand million exports in 1976, $30.80 thousand million were sent to the major industrial nations. The comparable figure for 1970 was $9.10 thousand million whereas in 1955 the developing countries collectively sent $1.90 thousand million to these nations. Thus, in value terms the expansion of industrial exports to the core regions has been somewhat slower than the over-all growth, but impressive nevertheless.

The periphery industrializes 97

The commodity structure of exports from developing countries is displayed in Table 20. Although textiles; clothing and 'other consumer goods' are important categories that account for much of

Table 20 *Manufactured exports from the developing countries, 1955–75 ($ thousand million f.o.b.)*

			1955	1970	1975
Oil-exporting developing countries					
C	Chemicals			0.04	0.53
Q	Textiles			0.13	0.32
U	Other manufactured goods	A	1.23	0.28	0.57
T	Total manufactures	B	0.04	0.45	1.40
		C	0.25		
Other developing areas		D	0.04		
A	Non-ferrous metals	E	—	3.56	4.19
B	Iron and steel	F	0.03	0.58	1.26
C	Chemicals	G	0.29	0.89	3.13
D	Consumer goods	H	0.17	0.33	0.83
E	Plastics	I	0.03	0.06	0.21
F	Wood semi-manufactures and paper	J	0.02	0.42	0.74
G	Other semi-manufactures	K	0.01	1.05	2.77
H	Engineering products	L	0.01	1.88	9.35
I	Agricultural and industrial machinery	M	0.07	0.14	0.65
J	Machine parts n.e.s.	N	0.01	0.19	0.68
K	Office and telecommunications equipment	O	0.01	0.27	1.97
L	Power generating machinery	P	0.01	0.17	0.77
M	Other engineering products and scientific instruments	Q	0.66	0.46	1.61
N	Road motor vehicles	R	0.08	0.11	0.70
O	Other transport equipment	S	0.31	0.13	0.75
P	Household appliances	T	3.05	0.41	2.22
Q	Textiles			1.88	4.52
R	Clothing			1.38	5.40
S	Other consumer goods			1.79	4.34
T	Total manufactures			13.45	35.70

Note: The countries of the world are grouped as follows: industrial areas, oil-exporting developing countries, other developing countries and the eastern trading area. New Zealand, Australia and South Africa are excluded from these groupings, but included in the world total.

Source: GATT (1978), Table A.3.

Table 21   *Commodity composition of manufacturing exports from developing countries, 1968 ($ million)*

	Commodity	SITC	Capital per man ($)	Exports from all developing countries ($ million)
1	Clothing	841	218	715
2	Non-cotton fabrics	653	435	293
3	Veneer, plywood	631	794	215
4	Cotton fabrics	652	748	195
5	Leather	611	443	139
6	Carpets	657	112	135
7	Toys and sports goods	894	252	123
8	Inorganic chemicals	513	4562	98
9	Pig iron	671	9095	91
10	Footwear	851	235	89
11	Organic chemicals	512	6160	84
12	Miscellaneous textiles	656	450	83
13	Radio receivers, etc.	724	1134	78
14	Textile yarn	651	748	68
15	Electrical machinery n.e.s.	729	1080	67
16	Articles of plastic	893	770	60
17	Essential oils, perfumes	551	520	52
18	Medicinal products	541	1903	46
19	Travel goods, etc.	831	640	42
20	Miscellaneous chemicals	599	4200	31
21	Other wood manufactures	632	1500	30
22	Special textile products	655	659	28
23	Office machines	714	1020	27
24	Fertilizer	561	9177	23
25	Jewellery	897	250	22
26	Iron and steel plates	674	9095	21
27	Furniture	821	738	16
28	Base metal household equipments	697	980	16
29	Iron and steel shapes	673	9095	15
30	Dyes n.e.s., tanning products	532	2160	14
31	Iron and steel pipes	678	2245	14
32	Rubber articles	629	3557	13
33	Plumbing, heating equipments	812	470	13
34	Cement	661	4230	11
35	Instruments and apparatus	861	3400	10
36	Tools	695	1554	9
37	Glass	664	2780	8

Table 21   *continued*

Commodity		SITC	Capital per man ($)	Exports from all developing countries ($ million)
38	Cutlery	696	420	8
39	Sound recorders, etc.	891	1134	7
40	Leather manufactures	612	640	7
41	Glassware	665	210	6
42	Paper and board	641	4000	6
43	Lace, ribbon, etc.	654	690	6
44	Plastic materials	581	7829	5
45	Watches and clocks	864	1575	4
46	Clay, refractory	662	1190	4
47	Non-metallic mineral manufactures	663	980	4
48	Pottery	666	498	3
49	Nails, nuts, etc.	694	1823	3
50	Domestic electrical equipment	725	500	2
				3059

Note: Non-ferrous metals and sugar are omitted.

Source: Mahfuzur Rahman (1973), pp. 109–10.

the growth, perhaps the most striking feature of this table is the wide spread of products and the prominence of engineering products collectively.

This extraordinary expansion of manufactured exports from the less developed nations was made possible by conditions in the core countries which persisted into the 1970s. Whether the conditions will be re-established after the recession which started in 1979 remains to be seen. Between about 1950 and 1973, the world economy expanded at an unprecedented rate. The core nations experienced labour shortages, which were not fully met by immigrant labour, partly because of ethnically based immigration policies (Seers *et al.*, 1979). Despite the rising proportion of women in the labour force, and despite the continuing application of mechanization, the shortage of labour invited the import of manufactures suited to labour-intensive and/or low-skill modes of production. To a substantial extent, the import of such goods was not a threat to the jobs of those working in Britain, Germany, the USA and other core nations. This was particularly because, with a high rate of over-all growth, adjustments in the economies of the core countries could be effected with relatively little individual hardship.

What, we may ask, is the basis for this remarkable growth of industrial exports from less developed countries? Although Mexico, Brazil and India have a varied resource base, the same cannot be said of Hong Kong, Singapore, Taiwan and South Korea. In any case, the pattern of industrial trade is not consistent with a high natural resource input. There seems to be little doubt that the key factor is labour supply. In a careful study, addressed to this very problem, Mahfuzur Rahman (1973) shows beyond doubt that the factor proportion approach is relevant. He disaggregated exports of manufactures from developing countries into fifty categories, and excluded non-ferrous metals and sugar, for which technological requiremennts make capital-intensive production a necessity. For his fifty industries, he examined the pattern of trade with the United States and Western Europe. As Table 21 shows, the total thus covered is about $3 thousand million, which is approximately one-third of the total manufacturing exports of all the developing countries in that year (GATT, 1978). However, the broad com-

Table 22 *Exports of manufactures from developing countries to developed countries, 1968*

Country	Population, 1970 (millions) (1)	Total exports ($ million) (2)	Total value added from manufacturing ($ million) (3)	(2)/(3) (4)
1 Hong Kong	4.0	910*	994	0.915
2 India	539.0	445	6812	0.065
3 Taiwan	14.8	250	807	0.310
4 South Korea	32.2	198	972	0.204
5 Mexico	50.7	191	7632	0.025
6 Pakistan	128.7	141	1353	0.106
7 Philippines	36.9	89	1102	0.081
8 Iran	28.7	85	921	0.092
9 Israel	2.9	68	1020	0.067
10 Argentina	23.7	66	6100	0.011
11 Brazil	92.5	64	5940	0.011
12 Jamaica	1.9	32	138	0.232

Table 22 *continued*

Country	Population, 1970 (millions) (1)	Total exports ($ million) (2)	Total value added from manufacturing ($ million) (3)	(2)/(3) (4)
13 Trinidad and Tobago	1.0	28	148	0.189
14 Singapore	2.1	21	168	0.125
15 Malaysia	10.4	16	363	0.044
16 Egypt	33.3	16	816	0.020
17 Colombia	20.5	15	1054	0.014
18 Morocco	15.5	12	360	0.033
19 Uruguay	2.9	10	390	0.026
20 Haiti	4.2	9	48	0.188
21 Algeria	14.3	8	429	0.019
22 Thailand	36.4	8	663	0.012
23 Panama	1.4	8	121	0.066
24 Nigeria	55.1	7	265	0.026
25 Tunisia	5.1	6	154	0.039
26 Chile	9.4	6	1080	0.006
27 Indonesia	119.5	4	1015	0.004
28 Venezuela	10.3	4	1425	0.003
29 Tanzania	13.3	4	60	0.067
30 Ghana	8.6	4	143	0.028
31 Peru	13.4	3	988	0.003
32 Dominican Republic	4.1	3	197	0.015
33 Paraguay	2.3	3	81	0.037
34 Kenya	11.2	2	143	0.014
35 Guatemala	5.3	2	240	0.008
36 Lebanon	2.5	2	219	0.009
37 Sri Lanka	12.5	1	238	0.008

Note: The ratios in column (4) give the relative importance of exports in total manufacturing activities of different countries, but the data in the two columns are not comparable.
* Re-exports account for about 20 per cent of Hong Kong's total exports but since the greater part goes to other Asian countries the figure shown here is not seriously affected.

Sources: Mahfuzur Rahman (1973), pp. 84–5; United Nations *Statistical Yearbook, 1978*, pp. 68–84; Fullard (1972), pp. 11–16.

modity structure shown in Table 21 is consistent with the data in Table 20. Mahfuzur Rahman's data show that manufacturing exports from developing countries to the core nations are, as expected, labour-intensive in character, with the major exceptions of veneer and plywood, which is a capital-intensive, resource-based industry, and jute-based products exported from Pakistan (now Bangladesh). As of 1968, six countries accounted for a very high proportion of total exports from the developing countries to the developed nations, as Table 22 shows. Nevertheless, several other countries, such as Israel, Argentina, Brazil and Jamaica are also significant exporters (Iran should probably be discounted, since her exports consisted almost entirely of rugs and carpets).

Two myths about this recent pattern of industrialization must be noted. First, because the export industries pay wages which are low by standards in Japan, America and Europe, one cannot say that the workers are being 'exploited'. Low wages reflect the inescapable fact that the opportunity cost of labour is negligible. With exceptions such as Hong Kong and Singapore, where agricultural opportunities are very limited, productivity in the agricultural sector is generally low. Until and unless productivity in farming is raised substantially, even very modest wages in factory employment will be attractive to many workers. The second myth is that multinationals have moved into the developing countries, in response to the availability of cheap labour, as part of the international pattern of their activities. Over all, in Latin America somewhat over 40 per cent of manufactured exports in 1966 was attributable to United States capital investment; the proportion was as high as 87 per cent in the case of Mexico and 42 per cent in Brazil, but lower elsewhere. For Asia as a whole, Morton and Tulloch (1977) estimate that only 10 per cent of industrial exports originated with foreign capital investment, ranging from 3–4 per cent for India to 30 per cent for Singapore, with Taiwan at 12–15 per cent. For the developing countries as a whole, Lal (1975) estimates that in 1967, 20 per cent of their manufacturing *output* – as distinct from exports – originated from capacity created by private overseas investment. However important multinational companies may be in the economies of the developing countries, it is quite evident that their industrialization cannot be ascribed primarily to the investment of these big firms within their borders. On the other hand, it does appear that manufacturing on a sub-contract basis is immensely important in the growth of exports. Sub-contract manufacturing accounted for about one-third of South Korea's industrial exports in 1969, and between 50 and 80 per cent of all Asia's exports (Morton and Tulloch, 1977).

The question arises as to why this new impulse for development is evident in some countries and not in others. It would be foolish to offer a simple explanation. However, it is notable that among the countries in Table 22, African nations are prominent by their absence; Latin America and Asia dominate the list. The Latin American states have been in the game far longer than the majority of Asian countries and, with the exception of India, have the largest aggregate manufacturing base. On the other hand, it is the Asiatic countries which have shown the most rapid growth in recent years.

It is unlikely that growth of manufactured exports to the core countries can continue at the tempo of the recent past for more than a few decades, since the proportion of the core countries' total imports that would then be accounted for would be sizeable. In any case, it is only for the *smaller* of the Third World nations that such exports can form the main propulsive basis for economic development. Were India, Mexico, Argentina and Brazil to raise the ratios in column (4) of Table 22 even to 0.250, the additional volume of goods entering the core countries would be very large.

For the future, we may visualize three distinct patterns of industrial development in the peripheral countries. Those with a relatively small population – less than, say, 10 million or 15 million – but possessing rich natural resources are likely to find it hard to develop export manufactures, other than those based on their resource endowment. The fundamental reason for this difficulty is the high opportunity cost of labour, which implies that industrial exports based on cheap labour is not a practicable option. New Zealand and Australia, with populations of 3 million and 16 million respectively, could be regarded as type examples, along with the oil-rich states. As an example of the industrial problems faced by this class of countries, the average effective protection for Australian manufactures in 1969–70 was 35 per cent, a level of assistance comparable to the levels recorded in Table 18 (p. 92) for selected developing countries (Parliament of the Commonwealth of Australia, 1976, p. 43). The oil-rich countries have experienced serious wage inflation in response to the massive inflow of funds, a phenomenon which proves a serious hindrance to general economic development. Paradoxical as it may seem, traditional modes of living persist alongside the modern economy, which in the Gulf States and Saudi Arabia in particular is dependent upon migrant labour from Pakistan and elsewhere. The small domestic market limits import substitution manufacturing. Therefore, unless these countries can make the leap to relatively high-technology industry, backed with large capital investment, it is unlikely that industrialization can ever become the mainstay of their economies. Such a leap is itself unlikely in the foreseeable future for the less developed (even though 'wealthy' states), since it implies a high level of education, training and skill. It will take several generations at least for these characteristics to be acquired in Africa, the Middle East and parts of Latin America and Asia (see, for example, El Mallakh, 1979, on the development of Qatar).

The second category is the small nation whose natural resource endowment is poor. Opportunities in agriculture are limited and the major asset is abundant labour willing to work for relatively low wages. The level of general education and skill that is required need not be very high. Under these circumstances, export industrialization is a feasible option. The relatively small total population of these countries implies that their output can never be a large proportion of world production. Therefore, there is the prospect of a reasonably permanent place in the world economic system. With the passage of time, the labour cost advantage is likely to dwindle and therefore it will be necessary to move into higher technology, more capital-intensive forms of manufacturing. To the extent that exports permit capital accumulation and the simultaneous enhancement of education and skills generally, Taiwan, South Korea and similar states can look forward to a reasonably prosperous future.

It is the third group of countries, with populations in excess of about 30 million, for whom the development problems may prove the most intractable. For a limited number, export of manufactures can be an important feature of their development (see Table 22, p. 100) but it will not be possible for many more countries with medium-sized populations, let alone larger nations, to join the league. Were they to try to do so, the problem of absorbing their products on the world markets would create such serious tensions that protective practices would almost certainly be employed severely to limit their exports. Since import substituting industrialization is limited by the low purchasing power of the rural population, the key to future prosperity in China, India, Pakistan, Bangladesh and Indonesia in particular must lie in raising the productivity of the agricultural sector, a matter to which we will turn in Chapter 5.

Technological diffusion

For the present purpose, we will accept the idea of the stock of scientific and technological knowledge as the common inheritance of mankind. That there are reasons seriously to doubt this proposition in certain contexts will become apparent in Chapter 5. Meantime, it provides the means to useful insight into some aspects of development, especially in the manufacturing field.

Most additions to the stock of scientific and technological knowledge originate in the more advanced nations which form the world's economic core. In the majority of cases, the early applications of useful new knowledge also occur in these same countries, from which there may be subsequent diffusion in appropriate cases. Viewing technological development as involving diffusion processes immediately raises two separate issues. First, there must be diffusion within nations, either of the new product or the new means for making an old product. Second, the new product or process must be transmitted from one nation to another.

We will not dwell on the first of these two diffusion processes. Since the publication in 1953 of Hägerstrand's seminal work on innovation diffusion, there has been a very large geographical literature published concerned with the problems of modelling intra-national diffusion processes. This literature has been admirably reviewed by a number of authors (Brown and Moore, 1969; Haggett, 1979; Cliff *et al.*, 1981). Virtually all of this work has been concerned with one of three kinds of innovation: the spread of diseases; the spread of new production processes among a large population of potential adopters – generally an agricultural technique spreading among farmers; and the spread of new goods and services among the population at large. So far as the present author is aware, no spatially based study has been published of the contemporary intra-national spread of an industrial manufacturing process.

In contrast, there has been some work done on the international diffusion of new manufacturing technology, both as new products and as new techniques for making old products. The difficulties inherent in the analysis of such diffusion are evident in the painstaking work of Nabseth and Ray (1974). Their study included ten new processes, ranging from the use of oxygen in making steel to the introduction of shuttleless looms. Altogether, six countries were considered – Austria, France, Italy, Sweden, United Kingdom and

West Germany. The year of the invention can be specified accurately, as can the year of first commercial application and the country in which this occurred. The date of first commercial application in each of the adopting nations can also be determined, giving the adoption lag. Thereafter, the concept of diffusion becomes less clear-cut. For their project, Nabseth and Ray measured the rate of intra-national diffusion in terms of the time taken from first introduction to the time when a specified proportion of national output was made by the new process. The proportion so specified varied from one process to another.

For the sample of processes and countries, it appears that there is an inverse relationship between speed of adoption and subsequent diffusion. In other words, the late adopters tended to catch up by converting to the new process more quickly than did countries quicker off the mark for initial adoption. This relationship is consistent with the idea that innovators and early adopters face technical and managerial problems that have been ironed out by the time the later adopters install the new equipment. With a maximum of ten observations for each of the six countries, no very meaningful figure can be obtained for each nation's mean lag. For what the figures are worth, the mean adoption lags were:

United Kingdom	2.3 years
Sweden	3.2 years
France	4.2 years
Austria	4.5 years
West Germany	5.1 years
Italy	6.2 years

The good performance of the United Kingdom is contrary to other evidence concerning the performance of that country's economy. Conversely, Germany's poor showing, along with Italy, is not consistent with the growth of her industrial capacity in the period following the second world war. Given the smallness of the sample, and the fact that all the countries are developed, it is not possible to draw general conclusions relevant for worldwide patterns of development.

A much more useful study in this context is that of Hufbauer (1966). He formulates a model of international trade along the lines of Figure 11. At time t_0, an innovation is first brought into use in the innovating country, initially to satisfy domestic requirements and

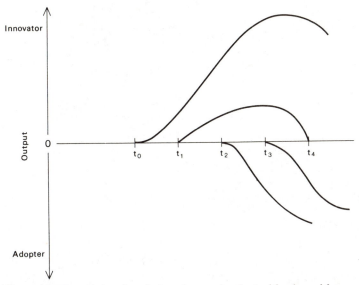

Figure 11   *International trade based on technological leads and lags*
Source: Hufbauer (1966).

then, from t_1, to supply export markets. At a subsequent date, t_2, production commences in the adopting country, initially as import replacement and then, from t_3, for export markets. As a result, the innovating country finds its export sales eroded and, in due course, may even find that its domestic sales are threatened by imports from the adopting country. This sequence of events is likely to be associated with the stabilization of technology for the given innovation, making it advantageous for plants to be established in countries where labour costs are relatively low.

Hufbauer explored these ideas in the context of the manufacture of and trade in synthetic materials. For this purpose he identified fifty-six materials and obtained data for selected years from 1910 to 1962. For each country an average lag can be computed as the mean of the lags for each commodity. Where a country is the innovator, the lag is zero. As an adopting country, the lag is the difference between the year of first production anywhere in the world and the year of first production in the country in question. Each commodity is weighted by its importance in world trade, measured by its tonnage (value figures were not available). A maximum aggregate imitation lag can also be calculated: for this purpose, the 'age' of

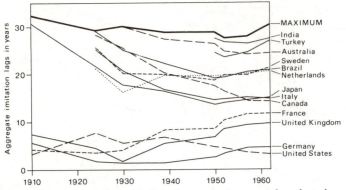

Figure 12   *Aggregate imitation lags for synthetic materials, selected countries*
Source: Hufbauer (1966).

each product, dated from the year of innovation, is weighted by its tonnage contribution to international trade.

Figure 12 summarizes Hufbauer's findings. In general, there has been some convergence of the imitation lags over the period 1910–62. The tendency for some of the core countries to be slower in adopting innovations may reflect the growth of the core itself and hence the dispersal of the sources of innovation. On the other hand, the trend to shorter lags for some of the peripheral countries must be a source of encouragement that, over a sufficiently long time-span, the worldwide distribution of leads and lags is mutable.

The world pattern of production and trade in synthetic materials is not determined by classical comparative advantage, since the localization of raw materials is not relevant. Hufbauer finds that the factor proportions theorem is inadequate in that wage differences between countries far exceed differences in profitability. Although scale economies and technological gap trade are evidently important, he is careful to note that it is impossible to determine which is the dominant consideration. For an industry which has been experiencing very rapid technological development, it is not surprising that low wages should be a relatively unimportant factor in world trade. Should this technological evolution slacken, then the factor proportions theorem would become more relevant. But perhaps the single most important point illustrated by the synthetic materials industry is the emergence of a new mechanism for international economic development to a prominence which was not evident in the nineteenth century, and that this mechanism does not necessarily concentrate all the benefits on the core nations.

Conclusion

As indicated at the beginning of this chapter, two competing views may be taken of the relationship of the core countries to the periphery. As Lewis (1978a, p. 16) remarks:

Our study originates from interest in the proposition that the upward movement of those already on the escalator helps to pull more and more countries into the moving company. This proposition is not obvious, and its opposite – that it is the enrichment of the rich that impoverishes the poor – is perhaps more widely held in one form or another.

Along with Lewis, I take the optimistic rather than the pessimistic view, and this chapter has argued why this is the appropriate stance to take. For the period 1870–1913, Lewis regards Britain, France, Germany and the USA as the world's economic core, wherein the primary engine of growth was industrial development. From this core, growth was transmitted to other countries through international trade, which for the peripheral countries was the (derived) engine of growth. As we have seen, since that time the core has expanded and its food and material demands have become a less powerful stimulus to development elsewhere. It is in fact necessary to disaggregate the periphery into a number of broad categories in order to identify the different kinds of growth process that now exist. Small countries which are rich in natural resources are unlikely to industrialize on a large scale, except for those industries where a resource location is desirable. Medium-sized countries with a substantial agricultural sector may be able to develop export industries on the basis of cheap labour. Countries with a large population will have to make progress with agricultural productivity if they are to achieve anything but a modest improvement in living standards.

Visualizing the world economy in terms of core and periphery, and concentrating on the processes whereby nations join the core or respond to it, Lewis explicitly argues in terms of the challenge posed by the core and the response of the periphery. In this respect, his mode of thought is similar to that of Toynbee (1934–59), though the nature of the challenge and response is different. As with Toynbee, Lewis asks why it is that some countries in some periods rise to the challenge, whereas others do not. In a book as brief as the present one, it is impossible to pursue these questions very far. However, as is implicit in the argument of Chapter 1, it is quite likely, almost certain indeed, that a long gestation is needed before rapid growth of a self-sustaining kind can get under way.

4 Non-renewable natural resources

The specter of a globe robbed of the material riches with which it once was amply blessed, has never ceased to prey upon people's minds. (Landsberg *et al.*, 1963, p. 8)

Economists and economic historians are probably inclined to underestimate the importance of natural resources in economic development.... (Youngson, 1967, p. 100)

Although there is always a minority of thinking men who are worried about the future availability of minerals and fuels, general concern seems to be episodic in nature. Present-day anxiety was triggered by the publication in 1972 of the Meadows report *The Limits to Growth*. Publication coincided with the latest upturn in the Kondratieff cycle (Rostow, 1978), i.e., with the beginning of a period when food and materials will probably be relatively scarce and expensive; since 1973–4, oil has certainly become suddenly and sharply dearer in real terms. Since 1972, there has been vigorous debate between those who take a pessimistic view of the future and those with a more optimistic frame of mind, a debate that has been usefully reviewed by Freeman and Jahoda (1978) and Manners (1981) among others.

Surveying the next fifty years, Manners rejects both outright pessimism and unfettered optimism regarding the supply of natural resource products. He settles for a guarded optimism, that supplies will remain available but at a price. In response to higher prices, he visualizes that strategies will be adopted to economize in the use of expensive commodities, to find substitutes and to recycle materials, in addition to active steps being taken to maintain or expand production. By these means, and given that there is now a real prospect of world population growth easing, there is no need to expect a catastrophic end to the process of economic development, although it is quite possible that the rate of growth which can be achieved worldwide may be slower than in the quarter century after the ending of the second world war. The qualified optimism expressed by Manners is a view shared by the present author. We will not enter the lists of the debate concerning the future survival of mankind. Our concern will be to examine some themes that, with limited exceptions (for instance, Crowson, 1979; Govett, 1976), have generally been overlooked or given little prominence in the literature that has appeared in recent years. We will focus on the geographical implications of relative scarcity and higher prices for fuels and minerals (Chisholm, 1977). This involves questions relating to the patterns of development associated with the exploitation of these resources and the transfer of capital and income from one area to another, both at the intra-national and international scales. Many minerals and fuels would not last for even half a century in the absence of further discoveries. In what seems to be a sober assessment, Eyre (1978) has compiled data for sixteen minerals and estimates that the median life of currently known reserves is twenty-nine and a half years; the range is ninety-eight years for chromium to a mere nine years in the case of gold. As a frame of reference, it is reasonable to postulate that for a very large number of non-renewable resources the presently known reserves will last no more than three decades.

One of the major characteristics of the industrial revolution was the substitution of inanimate sources of energy and materials for the products of farming and forestry as the basis for manufacturing (Wrigley, 1962a). Although in conventional national income accountancy terms fuels and minerals provide only a small part of the GNP of the major industrial powers, these economies could not now function without them. Worldwide, the production of primary goods has risen less rapidly than manufacturing output in recent years, but at about the same pace as population (Table 23). On the other hand, the volume of goods entering international trade has risen much faster than total output. Fuel, food and raw materials have shared in this expansion, though less markedly than manufactures. In value terms, ores, minerals and fuels collectively accounted for about 15 per cent of world trade in 1955 and 12.5 per cent in 1970. The tendency toward a declining share was sharply reversed with the rapid rise in oil prices that occurred from 1973, so that by 1976 ores, minerals and fuels accounted for 22 per cent of world trade (Table 24).

Whether in fact the world is entering a period of real scarcity of non-renewable resources or not, there is general agreement that for a very large number of minerals the currently known resources can

Table 23 *Trends in the quantum of world trade, 1948–77, compared with trends in population and production (1970 = 100)*

	1948	1958	1963	1971	1972	1973	1974	1975	1976	1977
Trade										
All commodities	22	38	54	106	116	131	137	132	147	153
Food and raw materials	36	55	73	104	112	126	122	121	132	135
Fuel	18	39	55	104	112	127	127	111	121	124
Manufactured goods	16	32	48	106	117	131	146	139	159	167
Population	67	80	88	102	104	106	108	110	112	114
Production										
Primary commodities	55	70	82	102	103	106	108	108	111	115
Manufactures	30	48	67	103	111	121	123	114	124	129

Source: United Nations *Statistical Yearbook, 1978*, p. 55.

Table 24 *Primary products in world trade, 1955–76, current values*

	1955		1970		1976	
	($ thousand million)	(%)	($ thousand million)	(%)	($ thousand million)	(%)
Total primary products	46.25	49.6	103.00	33.0	384.20	38.8
Ores and minerals	3.44	3.7	10.40	3.3	22.50	2.3
Fuels	10.26	11.0	28.67	9.2	195.80	19.8
World total trade	93.30	100.0	312.20	100.0	991.00	100.0

Source: GATT (1978), Table A.2.

last only for a matter of decades. New discoveries will undoubtedly extend the 'life' of these materials, and these new discoveries will probably change the geographical patterns of exploitation. Notwithstanding the elements of uncertainty, some important geographical implications can be derived with a direct bearing on the wealth of nations.

The regional distribution of resources

To the extent that the regional distribution of resources has been discussed in the debate on global supplies, three issues have predominated: the very high proportion of resources concentrated in the USSR, USA, Canada, South Africa and Australia; the prospective problems of maintaining the tempo of development in the industrial states which lack indigenous reserves; and the 'impossibility' of the less advanced nations replicating the pattern of production and consumption of the more advanced states for the want of the necessary fuels and minerals. It is the last of these propositions to which attention will be directed in this chapter, in conjunction with some related issues. The fundamental proposition is that if indeed scarcity marks the future, then given the unequal distribution of non-renewable resources across the world, at least some countries will be given an opportunity to embark on development on the basis of revenues from mining ventures.

Tables 25 and 26 summarize the present position for the major non-renewable fuels and minerals. In both cases, it is striking how the world's known reserves are concentrated in a very small number of countries, and that the five which have already been mentioned are prominent for the frequency with which they occur among the three or five major nations. This concentration reflects two factors. First is geological, there being no doubt that these five countries are exceptionally well endowed. In the second place, political stability has had an important role to play. The uncertainties surrounding politics and economic development in much of Latin America, Africa and Asia has been a serious impediment to exploration and exploitation. Thus, it is not altogether surprising that in the period 1970–3, 70 per cent of expenditure on mineral exploration in the market economies (i.e., excluding the USSR, Eastern Europe and China) took place in just four countries – the USA, Canada, Australia and South Africa (Bosson and Bension, 1977, p. 144). Therefore, it is almost certain that the presently known pattern of resources understates the relative importance of the less developed nations: for example, only 5 per cent of Indonesia has been mapped geologically and two-thirds of Burma remains to be effectively surveyed (Govett, 1975, p. 360).

Table 25 shows that the known coal resources of the world are concentrated in the USSR, USA and China in particular, with the

Table 25 *Regional distribution of proved recoverable and indicated additional reserves of coal and hydrocarbon fuels, c. 1978*

Fuel	Share of leading three countries	Share of leading five countries	Countries' percentage shares
Bituminous coal/anthracite	78.0	89.1	USSR (38.9), China (21.4), USA (17.7), Australia (7.9), West Germany (3.2)
Sub-bituminous coal/lignite	94.6	95.2	USSR (49.9), USA (37.9), Canada (6.8), China (0.3)*, West Germany (0.3)†
Total hydrocarbons	71.4	77.0	USA (43.9), USSR (18.1), Venezuela (9.4), Saudi Arabia (3.1)†, Iran (2.5)†

* Indicated additional resources only.
† Proved recoverable reserves only.

Source: World Energy Conference (1980).

Table 26   *Regional distribution of measured and indicated reserves, selected non-fuel minerals, 1977*

Raw material	Share of leading three countries	Share of leading five countries	Countries' percentage shares
Iron	59.4	76.7	USSR (30.2), Brazil (19.5), Canada (11.7), Australia (11.5), India (5.8)
Copper	44.9	58.7	USA (18.5), Chile (18.5), USSR (7.9), Peru (7.0), Canada (6.8), Zambia (6.4)
Lead	47.8	61.4	USA (20.8), Australia (13.8), USSR (13.2), Canada (9.5), South Africa (4.1)
Tin	50.2	68.1	Indonesia (23.6), China (14.8), Thailand (11.8), Bolivia (9.7), Malaysia (8.2), USSR (6.1), Brazil (5.9)
Zinc	45.8	58.6	Canada (18.7), USA (14.5), Australia (12.6), USSR (7.3), Ireland (5.5)
Aluminium	62.8	74.8	Guinea (33.9), Australia (18.6), Brazil (10.3), Jamaica (6.2), India (5.8), Guinea (4.1), Cameroon (4.1)
Titanium	59.0	74.1	Brazil (26.3), India (17.5), Canada (15.2), South Africa (8.6), Australia (6.6), Norway (6.4), USA (6.0)
Chromite	96.9	97.9	South Africa (74.1), Rhodesia (22.2), USSR (0.6), Finland (0.6), India (0.4), Brazil (0.3), Madagascar (0.3)
Cobalt	63.0	83.5	Zaïre (30.3), New Caledonia (18.8), USSR (13.9), Philippines (12.8), Zambia (7.7), Cuba (7.3)
Columbium	88.5	95.3	Brazil (76.6), USSR (6.4), Canada (5.5), Zaïre (3.8), Uganda (3.0), Niger (3.0)
Manganese	90.5	97.7	South Africa (45.0), USSR (37.5), Australia (8.0), Gabon (5.0), Brazil (2.2)

Table 26   *continued*

Raw material	Share of leading three countries	Share of leading five countries	Countries' percentage shares
Molybdenum	74.3	86.9	USA (38.4), Chile (27.8), Canada (8.1), USSR (6.6), China (6.0)
Nickel	54.5	76.8	New Caledonia (25.0), Canada (16.0), USSR (13.5), Indonesia (13.0), Australia (9.3), Philippines (9.0)
Tantalum*	72.7	84.8	Zaïre (55.0), Nigeria (11.0), USSR (2.9), North Korea (6.4), USA (6.1)
Tungsten	69.6	80.6	China (46.9), Canada (12.1), USSR (10.6), North Korea (5.6), USA (5.4), Australia (2.7)
Vanadium	94.9	97.2	USSR (74.8), South Africa (18.7), Chile (1.4), Australia (1.4), Venezuela (0.9), India (0.9)
Bismuth	47.9	60.9	Australia (20.7), Bolivia (16.3), USA (10.9), Canada (6.5), Mexico (6.5), Peru (5.4)
Mercury	65.2	78.3	Spain (38.4), USSR (18.2), Yugoslavia (8.6), USA (8.6), China (4.5), Mexico (4.5), Turkey (4.5), Italy (4.1)
Silver	54.9	76.5	USSR (26.2), USA (24.8), Mexico (13.9), Canada (11.6), Peru (10.0)
Platinum	99.5	99.9	South Africa (82.3), USSR (15.6), Canada (1.6), Colombia (0.3), USA (0.1)
Asbestos	81.3	91.8	Canada (42.7), USSR (32.3), South Africa (6.3), Rhodesia (6.3), USA (4.2)

* 1974 figures.

Source: OECD (1979), pp. 48–9.

Third World nations notable for their absence from the leading five nations. For hydrocarbons (oil, gas, oil shales, etc.), less developed nations are more in evidence, though America and Russia are again the two dominant states. In terms of current output, as distinct from reserves, the less developed nations occupy a much more prominent position in the international league. Indeed, international statistical tabulations now distinguish the 'oil-rich' developing countries from the others. Especially since 1973, oil prices have risen far faster than prices in general, resulting in a massive transfer of resources – a transfer so large that it has contributed to the recession experienced by the major industrial economies, created serious problems for the non-oil-rich developing countries, and generated grave balance-of-payments problems.

When we turn to non-fuel minerals (Table 26), the position becomes a good deal more complex. The relative importance of a few leading countries stands out, but numerous other nations, including poor and underdeveloped ones, also figure. If each country is scored one for each entry among the leading five in Table 26, then the most important states are:

USSR	17
Canada	13
USA	11
Australia	9
South Africa	7
Brazil	5
India	5

In addition, twenty-seven countries have scores of at least one, and a small number two, three or four. In some cases, it must be noted, the reserves are very small relative to the world's total, as with chromite in India. On the other hand, Chile has major reserves of copper and New Caledonia is well endowed with nickel. Virtually all the twenty-seven nations with scores between one and four can fairly be described as underdeveloped; for many of them, the scale of the mineral reserve is such that its exploitation has already had, or in the future could have, significant impact on the nation's development. Perhaps the most notable cases are Chile, New Caledonia, Peru, Zambia, Zimbabwe and Zaïre. These countries, and others among the two dozen or so that have at least 5 per cent of at least one major non-fuel mineral, have the potential to join the ranks of the present oil-rich nations, as possessors of highly valued resources which enable them to benefit from an international redistribution of wealth.

The *present-day* aggregate importance of non-fuel minerals in the economies of some countries is indicated by the following passage from a World Bank report, quoted by Crowson (1977, p. 14):

In Zambia non-fuel minerals account for more than 40% of GDP, in five other countries (Bolivia, Gabon, Liberia, Mauritania, and Surinam) they account for 25–30% and in three countries (Guinea, Guyana and Sierra Leone) for 15–20%. Non-fuel minerals account for a significant proportion of GDP in Chile, Indonesia, Jamaica, Mexico and Zaïre with a share of about 10%.

With the exception of Indonesia and Mexico, all the countries mentioned in this passage have small populations (under 15 million) and the majority are at an early stage in the development process. However, a large contribution to GDP from the mining sector does not guarantee rapid development, as the experience of Zambia indicates. For many years, President Kaunda was able to blame Zambia's flagging economy on the problems posed by UDI in Rhodesia. Legitimized independence for that country in 1980, as Zimbabwe, has exposed the long-term failures of Zambia's development. By contrast, the benefits of mineral exports have materially aided Mexico's successful progress since the last world war.

However great the opportunity which is afforded these countries, much will necessarily depend on the way in which the extractive industry is organized, the development processes which are associated with the extraction, and the proportion of the profit retained in the country which is host to the mining operations. This is an important matter to which we shall turn later (p. 138). Meantime, some consideration must be given to the process of development associated directly with the mining venture, and hence the prospect for long-term development at or near the mining site.

Resource-based development

In the literature both of geography and of economic history it is widely recognized that natural resources can provide the starting point for development. Geographers and regional scientists refer to the 'export base'; economic historians describe a similar process as the 'staple theory' of development. In essence, both terms describe the situation in which exports from a region or nation lead the growth process. The staple theory explicitly identifies natural products, such as fish, furs, minerals and agricultural products, as the export commodities which initiate development, and it is particularly associated with the Canadian economic historian Innis (1930, 1936); Caves and Holton (1959) use Innis' framework for their own study of Canadian development. However, as Watkins (1963) notes, the staple theory of development, formulated in terms of a settlement frontier moving into and across an area not previously inhabited by Europeans, is probably highly specific both in the time for which it is relevant and the appropriate geographical domain.

Export base theory is more general in concept, though focusing on intranational development rather than the growth of an entire national economy (North, 1955). In North's formulation, the impulse for development in a region arises from external demand for one or more locally produced goods. These may be agricultural in origin, forestry products or minerals, though North himself clearly was thinking of agricultural products in particular. He envisaged a cumulative process in which the extra local income arising from the export industry would generate a demand for goods and services that could be locally produced; the processing of the export staples would become more thorough (greater value added); infrastructure improvements would create opportunities for further development; and external scale economies would be realized, adding another twist to the upward spiral. As a concept of the development process, it is particularly applicable to areas which have already been settled but is not necessarily confined thereto. Furthermore, it is but a variant of the more general stages approach, which visualizes a progression from primary production to manufacturing and services. This view of development can be traced back at least to List (1885) and is recognizable in Clark (1940) and Seers (1970) among others.

Within this framework, minerals and fuels provide one class of export commodity, along with fisheries, forestry and agriculture. To understand the role, and the changing role, of non-renewable resources in economic development, it is necessary also to recall some fundamental ideas in industrial location. Weber (1929) formulated the principle of the least-cost location for an industrial plant and included in his analysis the idea of weight-gaining and weight-losing processes. If coal is used as a fuel, then although a substantial quantity will be used not a gramme will be added to the content of the final product. With a substantial loss of weight in processing, other things being equal it will be advantageous to locate the plant at or near the source of coal, to minimize the amount of tranport required. There may or may not be a loss of weight with respect to the other materials. The locational pull which is exercised by a fuel or raw material will depend on a complex interplay of several factors:

1 the degree of weight loss associated with the fuel or mineral;
2 the relative importance in the manufacturing process;
3 the structure and level of freight rates on the inputs and output;
4 the location of the raw material supplies and main markets.

Regarding the first of these variables, the general and quite striking trend over the last 150 years has been economy in the use of materials and fuels to achieve given ends. A dramatic example is provided by the consumption of coal in the manufacture of pig iron: five tonnes of coal were required for each tonne of pig iron in 1800–2 but only two tonnes in 1919 (Chisholm, 1966, p. 158). In 1910–14, one dollar value of raw materials and fuels yielded $4.3 of gross national product for the United States; by 1950, the equivalent figure was $7.2 (President's Materials Policy Commission, 1952). A similar trend has been identified for the industrial areas of Western Europe; between 1938 and 1954, gross manufacturing output for each £1 of raw material and fuel input rose from £4 to £5.6 (GATT, 1958). To some extent, the aggregate figures for the United States and Western Europe reflect changes in the economic structure, away from manufacturing and towards tertiary occupations. Nevertheless, economy in materials use has undoubtedly played a significant part. Furthermore, the trend has evidently continued, for the major industrial economies have managed to achieve more efficient use of oil to compensate for higher prices, to the extent of a 10 per cent reduction in consumption for a given level of economic activity.

That transport costs declined substantially relative to other costs, from the middle of the nineteenth century until well into the present century, is a generally accepted fact which has already been discussed (Figure 7 on p. 72, and pp. 81–2; see also Chisholm, 1979). As the network of modern transport systems has been filled in, the substitution of more efficient for less efficient transport modes has proceeded apace – from wagons, through canals to railways and roads. Simultaneously, the efficiency of each mode has improved faster than over-all economic efficiency, thereby reducing the real cost of transport and widening the range over which goods can be shipped economically. Finally, improvements in electric transmission have made possible yet another, though highly specialized, form of transport over long distances, as indeed has been the case with oil and gas pipelines. The steel industry illustrates the significance of these developments. Throughout the nineteenth century, international trade in iron ore was negligible. By comparison, in 1950 exports of iron ore accounted for just under 20 per cent of world production and by 1967 this proportion had jumped to almost 36 per cent (Manners, 1971, pp. 348–9). Much of this trade is accounted for by long-haul traffic, from Venezuela to the United States, and from Australia to Japan, for example. Similarly, Ion (1975) estimates that steam coal, exported from Alaska, Colombia, South Africa, Australia and China is shipped, on average, 6440 kilometres to its destination.

Two other developments should be noted in the present context. With the switch from coal to oil, gas and electricity, the energy content of fuels transported has risen sharply in comparison with coal. This implies that the unit cost of transport is likely to be lower than in the days of sole reliance on coal for use in furnaces and to raise steam. Second, technological developments have made possible the 'beneficiation' of many metallic ores at or near the mine. By the use of heat, flotation techniques or magnetism, much of the useless material can be eliminated and a highly concentrated ore is available for shipment. By virtue of the high content of useful material, these concentrates can be shipped great distances.

Perhaps the greatest monuments to resource-based economic development are the industrial regions of Britain, Western Europe, the USA and USSR which grew up on the coalfields in the nineteenth and early twentieth centuries. During this extraordinary period, several factors conspired to stimulate development in these areas. Rudimentary technology implied wasteful use of coal. In addition to coal, iron ore was often found interbedded, and clay was universally available for the manufacture of bricks, which became the principal building material. Transport was still costly and inefficient. Not surprisingly, as industrialization proceeded, migrants moved into the new industrial towns and the economic centre of gravity of nations shifted. This whole process has been well documented by Wrigley (1962b) for the major industrial zone of Europe, what he calls the Austrasian belt of coalfields running from northern France (Pas-de-Calais) to the Ruhr in Germany. For our purpose we must note two points in particular. First, as Wrigley points out, the coalfields had a long history of settlement and industry, though not based on the use of coal until about the middle of the nineteenth century. In other words, these were areas intrinsically favourable to human habitation on account of climate, terrain, accessibility and the availability of many local resources – ranging from water through farmland to forests. Second, with the decline and exhaustion of coal and the replacement of other resources (for example, iron ore) by imports, it has been possible for the major centres to adapt their economies and survive the cessation of the original enterprises.

Much the same has happened in Britain. The worst problems of adjustment to decline have been experienced in the upland margins of the Pennines, the valleys of South Wales, and in parts of Scotland. However, the permanence of Birmingham, Cardiff, Manchester and Newcastle-upon-Tyne is not in doubt, despite the sharp reversal of fortunes of the industries which resulted in the great nineteenth-century expansion. And, as in Western Europe, the big cities that grew up in the nineteenth century are located in areas which were previously occupied, even if not by cities of major standing for the period.

Part of the reason why Western Europe, and Britain in particular, was in the vanguard of industrialization lay in the availability of virtually all the necessary materials within, or very close to, long-settled areas with populations accustomed to trading and manufacturing. As Ashworth (1975, p. 54) comments:

For many years the task of keeping up adequate mineral supplies was among the more straightforward of those imposed by industrialization. The main need was to extract more of familiar materials in familiar places. As late as 1880 the three chief industrial countries, Britain, the USA, and Germany, with much smaller contributions from France and Belgium, accounted for all but a tiny fraction of the world's coal output, and major changes in the countries supplying other minerals were rare, though not unknown. As more was required it could often be obtained by carrying existing workings deeper or by starting new ones in the vicinity of those already in use....

In the late nineteenth century the situation was changed by the approaching shortage of some of the more familiar minerals in what had been the main producing districts and by the demand for new minerals that were not to be found in familiar places and were sometimes not obtainable at all by existing techniques of mining and quarrying. Activities in the old producing areas had already indicated one of the main ways to resolve the new problems, for in some of these, chiefly in Western Europe, the mid-nineteenth century had seen the inauguration of geological surveying on an extensive scale and this helped to make mineral prospecting a less chancy business. In the next fifty years the improvements of survey techniques ... and their application to many large areas previously of little commercial significance showed the existence of enormous and varied mineral resources. ...

Thus, as the nineteenth century wore on, the problem of material supplies was solved by extending the radius over which materials were shipped. This in turn was made possible by changes in transport and other technological developments, as noted above (p. 121). In this respect, the position differed markedly from the early stages of the industrial revolution. Then, as Wrigley (1962a,) persuasively argues, it was the substitution of inanimate materials for vegetable products, and particularly coal for wood and charcoal, that permitted industrialization to proceed without hitting the ceiling of development that would otherwise have been imposed by the impossibility of bringing adequate materials from vast distances, given the then existing technology of transport and manufacturing.

Reference to Tables 25 and 26 (pp. 115 and 116–17) shows that the major nations of Western Europe are not now well endowed with mineral and fuel resources in the context of global reserves. West Germany joins the top five for sub-bituminous coal and lignite, but this is the only appearance of any of the major European countries, although relative to her needs Britain is well endowed with gas, oil and coal. Europe now must rely on resources drawn from elsewhere. A similar prospect faces the USA notwithstanding that this country figures prominently in both Tables 25 and 26. Concern has been expressed ever since the 1952 report of the president's Materials Policy Commission. In 1900–4, mineral imports were approximately 10 per cent of home production, in value terms, and were equalled by exports. Since 1945, imports have ranged between 10 and 25 per cent of home production, whereas exports have amounted to only about 8 per cent. At the beginning of the century, there was over-all self-sufficiency, whereas by the end of the 1960s net supplies from domestic sources accounted for only 85 per cent of consumption (Cameron, 1973; see also Prestwich, 1975). Table 27 gives details of the import dependence of the USA, the United Kingdom, the other Common Market countries and Japan; over a large range of

Table 27 *Import dependence in the UK, EEC, USA and Japan, selected minerals*

| Mineral | Imports as a percentage of consumption Country or region | | | |
	UK	EEC	USA	Japan
Aluminium	62*	61*	85*	100*
Copper	82	81		90
Lead	46	53	4	76
Nickel	100†	100†	71	100
Tin	65	87	75	97
Zinc	100	<68	64	80
Iron ore	89	79	29	94
Manganese	100	100	99	90
Antimony	100†	95†		
Cadmium	81	36‡		
Chromium	100	100	91	100
Cobalt	100†	100†	98	
Niobium	100	100	100	
Germanium	100	100	35	
Mercury	100†	33	73	
Molybdenum	100	100		
Platinum Group	100†	100†	80	
Selenium	100	100	*c.* 42	
Tantalum	100	100	95	
Titanium	100	100		
Tungsten	99.5	> 99	54	
Vanadium	100	99	36	
Zirconium	100	100		
Uranium	100	59§		
Phosphate	100	99		100
Potash	57	20		
Sulphur	>87	>43		
Asbestos	100	100	83	100

Note: Figures are for 1974–6 for UK and EEC, 1974 for USA, and 1972 for
    Japan. Consumption includes secondary recovery.
* Allowing for imported bauxite, alumina and metal.
† Excluding scrap.
‡ Nearer 100 with ore.
§ Proportion will rise rapidly as EEC consumption grows and French
production provides a smaller percentage.

Source: Crowson (1977), Annex A.

minerals, foreign supplies meet all or a very large share of consumption. A time dimension to this position is provided by Table 28.

Several supply responses are possible to the evolving pattern of demand and changes in technology. One strategy is to push the search for minerals and fuels into ever remoter and less hospitable regions. Such a shift merely continues a process that has been going on for a long time, at both the international and intranational levels. While the search was confined to the more hospitable regions of the world, long-term development could be expected in the mining regions (Perloff *et al.*, 1960; Perloff and Dodds, 1963; Perloff and Wingo, 1964); this has become progressively less feasible. The extreme case is presented by the exploitation of the oceans, where long-term settlement is impossible. As Earney (1980, p. 36) notes, about 20 per cent of the world's petroleum production already comes from off-shore wells and the proportion may be as high as 50 per cent by 1990. We will explore the implications of this progressive shift in exploitation towards inaccessible and inherently hostile locations, initially by means of a simplified model of the development sequence.

Imagine two inhabited areas, both industrialized and developed, represented by A_1 and A_2 in Figure 13. Two versions of the spatial search process may be postulated. In the upper half of the figure,

Table 28 *Percentage production of selected minerals in countries which are now rich and poor, 1899 and 1974*

Mineral	Rich countries*		Poor countries	
	1899	1974	1899	1974
Iron ore	99	63	1	37
Copper	90	56	10	44
Lead	90	71	10	29
Zinc	—†	72	—†	28
Tin	13	13	87	87
Mercury	91	67	9	33

* Western and Eastern Europe (including USSR), USA, Canada, Japan, Australia, New Zealand.
† While statistics for zinc in 1899 are not available, it may be noted that only one of the seven main mining regions was in a poor country (Algeria).

Source: Freeman and Jahoda (1978), p. 174.

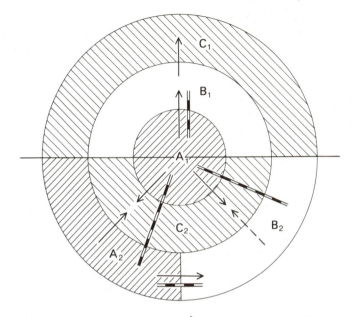

=== Road or railway　━ ━ ━>Direction of mineral search

Figure 13　*Schematic model of world mineral exploration and exploitation*

region A_1 is bordered by B_1, an area which might have either of two characteristics:

1 a settled population but at an early stage of economic development;
2 little or no habitation but nevertheless so endowed by nature that settlement is perfectly feasible on a substantial scale.

As the core region, A_1, experiences an increasing need to import minerals and/or fuels, the initial search will be directed towards B_1. This search may be associated with colonization, as with European emigration to America, Argentina, South Africa, Australia and elsewhere. Alternatively, it may be linked to colonial expansion; for example, the development of tin mining on the Jos Plateau in Nigeria and the copper belt of Zaïre–Zimbabwe. In both cases, it is likely that transport facilities will be built, either to give access to deposits which have already been located, or as part of the general development associated with agricultural, pastoral and forest activities. The building of such communications provides the occasion for two kinds of fortuitous discovery. First, the actual process of constructing roads and railways may lead quite directly to the discovery of unsuspected deposits, as with Sudbury and Cobalt, two of Canada's major mineral fields, found during the construction of the Canadian Pacific railway (Caves and Holton, 1959, p. 32). Then, once the route has been established, it provides a thorough-fare for casual travellers and serious prospectors, as well as an avenue for pastoral and farming settlers.

The pattern of mineral discoveries in Australia during the nineteenth century fits very closely the model described so far. In the words of Blainey (1970, p. 300):

The first condition for mineral discovery was accessibility. The early Australian metal-mining fields were in the south-east corner of the continent – the first area to be settled – and were found in moist and lightly timbered lands where sheep had long grazed. Most of the major discoveries made late in the nineteenth century were on the arid plains or in the mountain forests which were unfit for flocks and crops and were uninhabited until miners arrived. The accessible mineralized districts were developed first, and within those districts the more accessible mineral outcrops were usually discovered first; many lay within one mile of pastoralists' homesteads, shepherds' huts, and, above all, roads leading into the interior. Many important discoveries in northern Australia in the twentieth century show the same affinity with roads and, occasionally, with roadside hotels. The principle that human settlement hastens mineral discovery is visible in other countries: the first gold of the Witwatersrand was found on a farm and the first Californian gold rush was to an excavation made for a mill-race. The spread of rural settlement into mineralized regions not only increased the likelihood that someone would see any minerals outcropping above the surface, but also, more important, it eased and cheapened the task of developing mineral deposits. Nevertheless, the discovery of mining fields lagged unevenly behind the coming of the first shepherds, teamsters, or timber-cutters to a region. Australia's first major copper field was discovered about five years after the first sheep-owner settled in the vicinity, Australia's first major silver-lead field was discovered about fifteen years after sheep-owners settled in the area, and the discovery of the first important gold and tin fields lagged more than thirty years behind the arrival of the first sheep-owners in the area.

Accessibility was also vital for the discovery of mining fields which lay in arid or rain-forest zones where no farmer or pastoralist settled during the nineteenth century. The prospectors who penetrated those regions towards the close of the nineteenth century used the frontiers of pastoral settlement as supply bases and pushed inland in search of minerals. If they succeeded, the new field itself became a supply base, a stepping-stone from which other prospectors moved out. Most of the base-metal fields in the forests of western Tasmania and the gold fields in the semi-deserts of Western Australia were opened through a series of stepping-stones. Emphasis on the problem of access to mineralized areas in the interior of Australia, and indeed to most mining lands of the new world, cannot be made too strongly.

Beyond B_1 lies the inhospitable and uninhabited, or virtually uninhabited area C_1. Some discoveries may occur accidentally in pursuit of other resources, of which furs have historically been the most notable in Canada and Russia. However, this is the arena which has been opened up to reconnaissance survey by modern geological prospecting techniques within the last half century or so – the wilderness of the northern tundra and the great deserts of the world.

An alternative sequence of events is suggested in the lower half of Figure 13. In this case, the core area of A_1 is bounded by an inhospitable wilderness (C_2), beyond which is another inhabited and developed region (A_2) and/or an underdeveloped region (B_2). In the first instance, a line of communication across C_2, to either A_2 or B_2, may provide the occasion for accidental discoveries. The case of Sudbury and Cobalt actually arose from this variant of the model, not the first. The development of B_2 may occur from either or both A_1 and A_2, and the exploration of C_2 may proceed from A_1, A_2 or B_2 – or from all three areas.

There is no doubt that over the last century the importance of C_1/C_2 locations has risen sharply, in both absolute and relative terms. The case of off-shore oil has already been mentioned (p. 126). Unfortunately, it is impossible to give general quantitative information of mineral exploitation in relation to environmental suitability for permanent large-scale settlement, and we must be content to piece together some fragments of information. With respect to petroleum and gas, there has been a striking shift in the location of main production sites between 1888 and 1978 (Figure 14). From ten areas in 1888, all located in reasonably hospitable environments, production has spread to over 100, many of which are unattractive on account of cold or drought, or totally uninhabitable on a permanent basis (for example, the North Sea). Northern Alaska, the northern Sahara desert and the deserts of the Middle East are producers of major importance, but none of these production sites is likely to prove convenient for large-scale, permanent settlement. Within Canada, there has been a marked northward movement of mining into the harsh environment of the Canadian Shield. Geological exploration of the Shield only began in 1842, with the organization of the Geological Survey of Canada, and considerable impetus was given by the construction and, in 1885, opening of the Canadian Pacific Railway. By the beginning of the second world war, the Shield accounted for the whole of Canada's nickel, radium, platinum and cobalt output, 86 per cent of copper, 85 per cent of gold and 38 per cent of silver (Department of Mines and Resources, 1947). That the northward movement of mining has continued is attested by the evidence presented by Armstrong and others (1978), though the spatial disaggregation of data below the level of Province presents real problems. For the USSR, however, the position is vividly illustrated by the following figures. Defining the 'north' of the country as the lands northward of 60°N in the European part of Russia and 50°N in the east, the only mineral mined in the north prior to 1917 was gold. By 1978, the following percentages of national production came from the north:

Gas	13	Tin	50
Oil	30	Nickel	66
Gold	45	Diamonds	100

In addition, phosphatic fertilizer output is important, about 10 per cent of aluminium comes from the north, and though only 4 per cent of iron ore is mined in the north the region's known reserves are very large. Though unworked, the country's largest copper deposit is also located in these boreal lands.

Australia reveals something of the same problem. Figure 15 locates all investment projects costing A$5 million (approximately £2.5 million) or more; above this threshold, the majority of investments are in the mining sector, not manufacturing, and of those that can be classed as manufacturing the greater number are associated with mineral extraction. Australia is a notoriously dry continent and even many of the projects around the eastern seaboard are in areas where water supply problems render large-scale, permanent settlement unlikely. For example, the companies responsible for the Queensland coal mining ventures are not setting out to build complete towns for their workers. In practice, provision is rudimentary, being designed for male colliers, among whom the turnover is high. Reviewing the over-all pattern of Australian

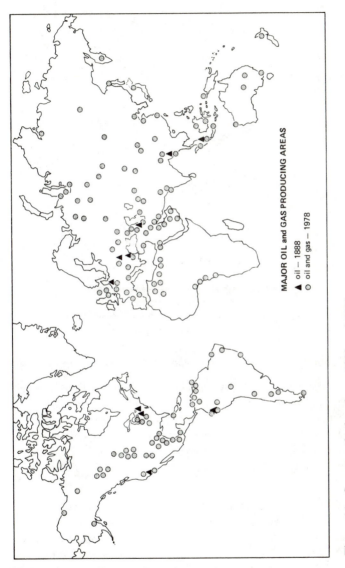

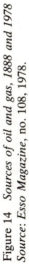

Figure 14 *Sources of oil and gas, 1888 and 1978*
Source: Esso Magazine, no. 108, 1978.

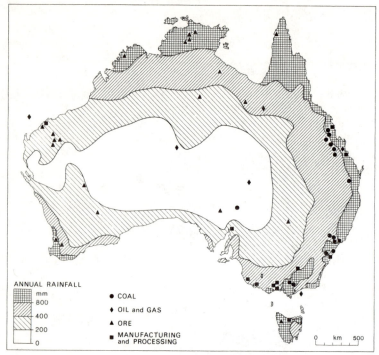

Figure 15   *Major capital investments in Australia for the 1980s*
Source: *Bank of New South Wales Review*, no. 33, 1980.

mineral development, *The Times* (4 December 1980) had this to say:

If 10 years ago you had asked Australians whether minerals might be the
key to their country's future the reaction would have been sceptical. Most
people believed that the main deposits had already been located and few
thought that Australia would or should allow its future to be determined by
activities as unfashionable then as geological exploration and large-scale
mining in remote, semi-desert places. They could not have been more
wrong.

At this juncture it is useful to take up a thesis developed by
Bradbury (1979). He examines the problems of 'resource-based
settlements' in Canada, i.e., settlements created for the purpose of
extracting a particular mineral or suite of minerals. An example is
provided by Schefferville, located 515 kilometres due north of the
port of Sept-Iles, in the heart of the Labrador–Ungava peninsula.

This particular iron ore mining community comprises 770 permanent family dwellings and 110 housing units on a trailer park; construction was completed in 1955. As with many similar communities, there are major problems concerning the adequacy of shopping, recreational and social facilities, i.e., about the quality of life. As a one-resource, one-company town, it is highly dependent upon conditions elsewhere in the world and company decisions taken at distant headquarters. Among other things, this means that the township can be abandoned, as has happened with the firm INCO at Sudbury, Ontario, and ASARCO at Buchans, Newfoundland. Bradbury regards this as evidence of 'dependency' and 'unequal development' in a capitalist economy dominated by multinational companies:

An adequate theory of resource-based town development depends upon an understanding of both the process and the context of capital accumulation and uneven development in the phase of historical capitalism being examined. (Bradbury, 1979, p. 147)

At no point does Bradbury consider the environmental circumstances and the inherent prospect for permanent, large scale settlement. Yet, as long ago as 1936, Innis drew attention to the transient nature of mining towns: between 1901 and 1921, the population of Yukon fell from 20,000 to 4000, in response to the exhaustion of gold deposits and the lack of other occupations in the locality – agriculture, for example, being confined to cabbages and potatoes for local use. In the year 1978, in the whole of the Canadian North, there were only 76,000 inhabitants, living in ninety-three communities. Of these settlements, only twelve exceeded 1000 people, and the only 'urban' places were Whitehorse (13,300) and Yellowknife (10,000). The majority of these very small communities have a very restricted and fragile economic base. Problems of the same kind are experienced in the Soviet Union, a major 'noncapitalist' economy. Murmansk is the largest northern city, with 300,000 residents, and four others exceed 100,000. However, away from these and a few other main centres, many settlements are much less permanent. Indeed, some are organized on the principle of workers spending up to two weeks at a time working continuously, living in hotel-like complexes. Periods of leisure between the spells of work are spent in larger, more permanent settlements elsewhere in the northern latitudes. Under these circumstances, the facilities for transient workers at the site of mineral extraction or other activity will be abandoned when the resource in question has been exhausted (United Nations, 1980).

Pushing exploration for minerals into ever remoter areas implies that initial capital costs must rise substantially, notwithstanding the offsetting effects of technical improvements in the exploration process. Although there is some dispute about the precise magnitude of this rise in costs, the direction of change and its approximate tempo is not in doubt. For example, Bosson and Bension (1977) state that in 1946–50 mineral exploration in Canada cost US$1 for every $155 discovered, whereas by 1966–70 the value of finds had fallen to only $50. On the other hand, McAllister (1976) cites figures which indicate a somewhat higher ratio in the late 1960s and a less rapid decline over the preceding one or two decades. The absolute cost of making a major mineral find is now quite considerable. Australia is a relatively unexplored continent and in the early 1970s a major find required about US$12 million of expenditure. By comparison, in Canada the figure was $30 million and in the US even higher, reflecting the longer period of active exploration and development in these countries than in Australia. For the international petroleum industry, exploration costs off Labrador and Greenland, impeded by ice floes, are ten times higher than costs in the North Sea and twenty times greater than in Saudi Arabia (Earney, 1980, p. 159). Indeed, Parra (1980, p. 3) considers that the general cost of obtaining incremental oil resources may be twenty to thirty times the average cost of Middle East oil.

Once a find has been fully proved and the decision taken to exploit it, additional and very substantial capital expenditure will be required – to prepare the mine and its supporting services and also the means for evacuating the fuel or ore for sale elsewhere. This last cost can be immense if distances are great and/or the terrain difficult – as with the construction of the trans-Alaska oil pipeline. According to Freeman and Jahoda (1978), in 1975 there were thirty-nine non-fuel mineral projects in the world outside Eastern Europe and the USSR with a total capital cost of over $400 million each. Of these, eighteen involved capital costs in excess of $600 million, and for two the figure exceeded $2000 million. To put these thirty-nine projects into perspective, note that 70 per cent of the world's metal production come from just 170 mines. For the western world, 90 per cent of metal output requires no more than about 1000 mines. There seems to be little doubt that the problems arising from remoteness and inhospitable environments have materially contributed to the general rise in capital costs noted by Crowson (1977).

For a project of any size, the construction phase will last for several years, even a whole decade, before production is possible. This puts considerable pressure on the cash-flow balance and provides a substantial spur to achieve high output levels shortly after productive operations begin. In the case of the North Sea, Earney (1980, p. 69) gives the following figures for the time and cost of finding and developing an oil field:

Phase	Duration in years	Capital investment US $ millions	Operating costs 1973 prices
Exploration	2–6	24–147	
Construction	5–6	612	
Production	16–20	122–245	612–735

To appreciate the significance of high capital costs prior to production, it is useful to rehearse very briefly the basic principles of discounted cash flow accountancy. Table 29 presents some hypothetical data for an investment project. We assume that the present is represented by time 0 and, for simplicity's sake, that expenditure and revenue both come in discrete lumps at the end of the first, second, third, etc. years from now onwards. We will further assume that there is no inflation. Over the first four years, investment builds up to its maximum annual rate of £2 million. As production operations commence in the fifth year, investment falls off and from the sixth year onwards outgoings settle at the regular costs of operation, £0.5 million per annum. Over the ten-year period, total costs amount to £9 million. The time-flow for receipts is very different. There is no income until the fifth year, from which time revenues build up quickly to their peak in the seventh year. Over the ten-year period, total revenues amount to £11.8 million, which appears to be comfortably in excess of expenditures. However, the differential time-flow of outlays and revenues must be taken into account. Just in the way that £1 invested in the bank today will accumulate interest and be worth more one year hence, so the present value of future expenditure or revenue can be calculated by applying a rate of interest in reverse, i.e., by discounting. At 10 per cent interest, £1.00 today is worth £1.10 one year hence; conversely,

Table 29   *Hypothetical data to illustrate discounted cash flow*

Year	Expenditure (£ million)			Receipts (£ million)		
	Current value	Present value*	Accumulated present value*	Current value	Present value*	Accumulated present value*
0 (=present)						
1	0.5	0.45	0.45	0	0	0
2	1.0	0.83	1.28	0	0	0
3	2.0	1.50	2.78	0	0	0
4	2.0	1.37	4.15	0	0	0
5	1.0	0.62	4.77	1.0	0.62	0.62
6	0.5	0.28	5.05	2.0	1.13	1.75
7	0.5	0.26	5.31	4.0	2.05	3.80
8	0.5	0.23	5.54	3.0	1.40	5.20
9	0.5	0.21	5.75	1.0	0.42	5.62
10	0.5	0.19	5.94	0.8	0.31	5.93
Total	9.0	5.94	5.94	11.8	5.93	5.93

* Assuming interest at 10 per cent per annum.

£1.10 in twelve months is 'worth' £1.00 now. For the purpose of constructing Table 29, a ten per cent rate of interest has been assumed and the current values converted to present values, on which basis this particular project, instead of making a profit, just breaks even. Each year's delay in obtaining revenue adds a substantial penalty in terms of reduced present value of the income. Furthermore, at any rate of interest that can now be regarded as reasonable, any revenue beyond year twenty is of negligible value. For example, at 10 per cent interest, a revenue of £1.00 in the twentieth year has a present value of only £0.149, or 15 per cent of the nominal value.

Great complications are introduced by general inflation and the prospective behaviour of commodity prices. If these are expected to rise very rapidly in the future, there may be a case for keeping the appreciating asset in the ground. Nevertheless, it is generally true that the higher the initial capital costs, and the longer before any revenue is obtained, the greater the pressure for the highest possible output at the earliest opportunity. Thereby, all other things being equal, the resource will be exhausted more quickly than a similar deposit requiring lower capital investment.

Whatever the global position may be regarding aggregate consumption and total reserves, ransacking the wilderness implies ever-increasing capital costs and hence a shorter working life for each reserve that is exploited. Exactly the same argument applies to the effects of deeper mines and wells. The only general way in which this tendency could be offset would be through the discovery of progressively bigger deposits. Eyre (1978) selected eleven non-ferrous metals and identified the twelve main producing sites (mines or groups of mines) in the year 1973. Of a total of 131 sites in the non-communist world, he was able to identify the date of earliest working in forty-nine cases. Over a time-span from pre-1500 to post-1960, there is no clear tendency for the biggest mines to have been started recently. The main periods of starting new mines are the decades 1880–90 and 1930–40, these being the decades in which the largest numbers of these major mines began to produce. This evidence is consistent with the findings which have already been cited, that the value of discoveries relative to the cost of exploration has been falling (p. 134), although Bosson and Bension (1977) note that in Canada this rising cost has been partially offset by an increase in the size of discoveries. Experience in the USA has seen a fall of about 40 per cent in the average size of finds in the period 1955–9 to 1965–9. So far as petroleum is concerned, it appears that the view expressed by Adelman in 1964 remains true. In a section entitled 'The Middle East as a huge random disturbance', he notes that only in 1944 was the magnitude of the region's oil resources first fully realized, and that its size is such that it could not have been predicted as a possibility given the size-distribution of previous finds. Nothing comparable has since been located.

The safest conclusion that we can draw from the foregoing discussion is that any increase in the size of future finds is unlikely fully to compensate for the rising costs of discovery and development. The implications which follow from this conclusion are reasonably clear. First, it is evident that the exploitation of minerals and fuels has now moved into very inhospitable parts of the world which inherently do not lend themselves to permanent settlement on a large scale. Throughout northern Siberia, northern Canada and Alaska, and the major deserts, agriculture is virtually impossible, except under peculiar circumstances such as the availability of fossil groundwater, which in Libya is being used for irrigated cropping. With meagre means of livelihood available, other than the specific resource being exploited, settlement is almost by definition limited to the duration of the mining operation, which itself is likely to be relatively short lived.

Especially in Third World countries, mining operations may and do occur in areas which are reasonably habitable but where the population may be sparse, and the level of economic development is in any case low. The technological gap between the host community and the mining enterprise will be great, much greater than was the case in the nineteenth and early twentieth centuries in Western Europe and America. This is the traditional feature of the 'dual economy', or 'enclave' development. Our understanding of this is crucially affected by the time horizon. If, as we have argued, the life of individual mining enterprises is getting shorter, there is a decreasing amount of time in which linkages and multipliers can operate in the vicinity of the mine. The traditional pattern of development, in which a permanent population will remain after the resource has been exhausted, able to turn its energies to other forms of productive enterprise, is of diminishing utility.

The small size of actual *local* multiplier effects has been noticed in a number of studies, of which the collection of essays by Mikesell *et al*. (1971) is one of the more thorough. The case studies presented refer to several extractive operations that had been in progress for many decades, including sulphur in Mexico and copper in Chile. Some of the mining operations are located in areas that are inherently inhospitable (for example, oil in Saudi Arabia and copper

Table 30 *Percentage of mineral exploitation retained value attributable to wages paid locally and local purchases*

Country	Mineral	(%)
Venezuela	Petroleum (1950–64)*	21.8–42.1
	Iron ore (cumulative, 1951–67)	53.1
Iran	Petroleum (1966)	28.9
Saudi-Arabia	Petroleum–Aramco (1966)	9.8
Chile	Copper (1930–39)	79.3
	(1940–54)	69.4
	(1955–64)	51.5

* The proportion declined from about 40 per cent in the early 1950s to about 25 per cent in the early 1960s.

Source: Mikesell (1971), pp. 130, 232, 244, 339, 417.

in Chile) but elsewhere, as with iron-ore mining near Belo Horizonte in Brazil, the environmental conditions can be described as reasonable. Table 30 has been culled from the studies by Mikesell and his colleagues; it shows two things of particular note. First is the wide variation in the proportion of the retained value that is represented by wages and local purchases, and which potentially may stimulate permanent development in the vicinity of the mining enterprise. The data in Table 30 refer to the value retained within the country, which implies that some – perhaps much – is spent far away from the mine itself. For the two cases where time-series data are available (petroleum in Venezuela and copper in Chile), the proportion spent on wages and local purchases has been declining. There is every reason to suppose that this decline is representative of general and continuing experience. The balance of the retained value comprises taxes, profits on currency dealings and other revenues accruing to central government funds. Reviewing the evidence of the case studies, Mikesell (1971, p. 25) concluded that the extractive industries:

have little direct impact on the course of development in the host countries since they engage only a small portion of the domestic labor and capital and of land having alternative uses. Their indirect impact on both the rate and pattern of social and economic change may be enormous, but this depends upon governmental policies in allocating revenue and in providing induce-ments to broadly based development, on the one hand, and upon the ability of society generally to utilize the returns from the subsoil for maximum social and economic progress, on the other.

This position cannot be attributed to the specifically self-seeking operations of multinational companies. In large measure their behaviour is determined by the circumstances under which they work. The scale of modern projects is such that they can only be undertaken either by governments or by large, usually multinational companies. Even a country as rich as Australia cannot generate enough capital for all the investment in the manufacturing and mining sectors. Private capital inflow throughout the 1970s amounted to A\$975 million annually (approximately £500 million per annum). During the mid 1970s, foreign investment in mining accounted for between 42 and 49 per cent of total investment in that sector. In order to finance a large programme of mineral, fuel and manufacturing projects during the 1980s, it is expected that the annual capital inflow will have to rise from about A\$1 thousand million to about A$4 thousand million in the early years of the decade. This inflow may be compared with *total* private investment in Australia of about A$8 thousand million per annum (1980), which itself is twice the volume of investment only four years previously. (*Bank of New South Wales Review*, 1980).

All governments of countries which are host to multinational companies, whether they be in the manufacturing or extractive sectors, are faced with the same fundamental problem. How to attract the initial investment, and how to obtain the maximum benefit from the operation. That the core nations of the world are caught up in this problem just as much as the nations of the periphery is evident from attitudes in a country such as Britain towards the operations of multinational companies. Development of the oil resources of the North Sea has depended very largely on foreign capital and successive governments have done their best to maximize exchequer revenue from the operations while at the same time ensuring that the structure and level of taxes does not deter continuing exploration and development. Towards the end of 1980, the government were considering what adjustments should be made to increase the public 'take', given that high oil prices were allowing the companies to make much larger profits than had been expected. Britain is also host to large multinational companies in the manufacturing sector. There are some who believe that the operations of these companies are detrimental to regional interests, if not also to the nation as a whole (Holland, 1976), but this viewpoint takes little account of the over-all realities of the situation.

It may be argued that the core nations have greater bargaining power with multinational companies than do the less developed, peripheral nations. Generalizations of this kind do not seem appropriate. Much more important, especially for resource projects, is the sophistication with which host nations negotiate with the multinationals. The last twenty years or thereabouts has witnessed the success of the oil-exporting countries in determining the terms on which crude oil will be available, whereas previously the major oil companies had things pretty much their own way. If, as seems probable, we are now at the start of an upswing in the Kondratieff cycle, which may be superimposed on a secular trend toward resource scarcity, then the bargaining position of resource owners will improve over the next generation or so. Although inevitably with differing success, it seems reasonable to postulate that nations with a surplus endowment of minerals and fuels will be able to effect a transfer, probably a sizable transfer, of resources in their direction. Exploration licences, production royalties, profit taxes, etc., all provide the means whereby substantial revenue to government funds can be obtained.

That this is now the main significance of mineral developments has been recognized by a number of authors. In the early history of Canada and throughout the nineteenth century, mineral deposits provided foci for permanent settlement, as Caves and Holton (1959, p. 45) make clear:

With the history of settlement largely a closed book their significance shrinks beside the meaning which these developments hold for the *aggregates* of Canadian income, production and trade. Thus E. S. Moore, summing up the significance of Canadian mining in the 1930s stressed the number of jobs dependent on mining. One-seventh of Canada's population, he concluded, depended for support on workers employed directly in mining or indirectly in processing, transportation, and distribution of the products of mining activity. These facts now hold much more significance for the economy than the local impact of changes in mining activity on the patterns of settlement.

Conclusion

In this chapter, we have reviewed what may seem to be a rather specialized topic. However, when the discussion is viewed in the context of previous chapters, the central issue is abundantly clear. Viewed over a century or similar time period, we can identify different impulses for development. While the traditional role of minerals and fuels as the site for development declines in importance, in the sense that *in situ* development on a large scale becomes less relevant, nevertheless the world's demand for non-renewable resources is opening up opportunities for a significant number of smaller countries and some medium-sized ones. The possibility is provided for yet more countries to join the ranks, if not of the developed, at least of the rapidly developing nations. However, the opportunity is likely to be a once-only chance, that may not be repeated. Because the traditional processes of cumulative private investment in the region of mining are less relevant than hitherto, governments cannot afford to sit back and wait for events to unfold. Active participation by governments throughout all stages from initial exploration licensing to the taxation of profits and the reinvestment thereof, is necessary if the opportunity is to be seized. For those that can rise to the challenge, the rewards may be considerable. Failure implies the prolongation of poverty, conceivably for many generations. Given the extreme contrast that exists in many countries between the traditional economy and modern ways of doing things, and the poverty of complementary resources in some cases (for instance, the states of the Persian Gulf), the transition is likely to be difficult, not least because of the rapidity with which it must be effected.

5 The populous less developed countries

A foreigner is walking on a tightrope when he is called upon to advise or work in such fields as community development, agriculture, education and other social activities. (Onyemelukwe, 1974, p. 112)

Throughout the greater part of the modern era, until after the second world war, it has been customary to regard the total population of a country as an exogenous variable, beyond the influence of governments. The most important exception to this prevailing view has been the group of European-settled countries receiving a sustained net migration inflow. From the early 1920s, immigration controls became general, in particular for the USA, Canada, Australia and New Zealand. In part, the intention was to impose ethnic selection to minimize or obviate the risks of racial conflict and the supposed danger of 'diluting' the genetic stock; the 'white Australia' policy was the most clear-cut on this issue but a similar idea underlay America's imposition of immigration quotas by nationality of origin. A second reason for immigration controls was to keep out individuals deemed undesirable because of infirmity or a criminal record, irrespective of their nationality. Third was the desire to regulate the rate of growth in total population, so that numbers would not exceed the work available.

Prior to the ending of the second world war, we otherwise note the encouragement given in Italy, Germany and Russia in particular to parents with large families. The motivation had much to do with military considerations, and echoed the 'populationist' attitudes of the eighteenth century. Quite what the impact of favourable publicity, generous maternity benefits, the provision of nursery and school facilities, etc., was on the demographic experience of these countries is a moot point. In the present context, it is more important to note that the policies pursued by this limited number of countries were distinctly untypical.

Since 1945, attitudes to both migration and net reproduction have changed substantially. Involuntary migration on a significant scale occurred in the aftermath of the war, notably German refugees fleeing westward. The granting of independence to India and Pakistan was accompanied by communal violence and very large population transfers. Elsewhere political independence for former colonies triggered the expatriation of 'colonials' to the motherland – from Algeria to France, from Indonesia to Holland, and from Mozambique to Portugal. In addition, local wars in Vietnam and Kampuchea, for example, have driven many thousands to seek refuge in safer places. Permanent population transfers were at a peak in the 1940s and 1950s. Thereafter, there has been a continuing serious refugee problem in many parts of the world, though it is difficult to know the numbers involved and the degree of permanence of the population transfers. For our purposes, we will regard involuntary migration as an episodic interruption to the more usual pattern of international migration.

Voluntary migration between countries is now on a much smaller scale than at its peak in the nineteenth and early twentieth centuries. Most countries now exercise careful control over immigration, both to limit the total population and to minimize problems of ethnic conflict. The documentation of international migration leaves much to be desired. The 1977 edition of the United Nations *Demographic Yearbook* contains a detailed tabulation of the available statistics for recent years up to 1976. For many countries, emigration and immigration data are not available, and for those for which they are difficulties of comparability, of definition and coverage are serious; for example, the Swiss data for long-term emigration refer only to males. Nevertheless, figures for long-term emigration can be aggregated for sixty-four countries, for the year 1976 or some recent but earlier year. The total emigration in one year thus recorded is 1.35 million, which compares with the estimated resident population in the same countries of 968.65 million in 1976. For this sample of countries, representing just under one-quarter of the world's population, the annual number emigrating is equivalent to only 0.14 per cent of the estimated inhabitants. Since it is known that there is very little emigration from the Soviet bloc, China, the countries of the Indian sub-continent and Indonesia (all excluded from the above figures), the probability is that the worldwide volume of emigration is no higher than 0.14 per cent per annum, and probably less, and therefore less than about 5 million in total each year.

Given the low level of international migration, the main determinant of total population for practically all nations is the level of net reproduction. Until relatively recently, the view was widely held that governments could not effectively intervene to limit the rate of population increase. Consequently, for virtually all the developing nations of the Third World, population growth was treated as an exogenous variable, beyond government control. Consequently, in drawing up plans for development, the rulers of China, India, Nigeria and many other countries have derived from population projections target levels of food supply, manufacture of consumer goods, house construction targets, etc. In other words, over-all economic growth had to match the rate of population expansion, with something to spare so that resources could be provided to achieve specified goals. Since population typically increases by 2 or 3 per cent annually, or even faster, governments have found that the rate of economic growth that must be postulated has exceeded what can be achieved in practice. Indeed, in some agrarian societies the expansion in the number of mouths to be fed has led inexorably to the sub-division of farms, over-cultivation and the degradation of the land – so confounding the hopes for higher total output. From the late 1960s onwards, governments have been forced to reconsider their attitudes to population growth. In this they have been materially aided by the rapid post-war evolution of contraceptive technology. With the multiplication of the means for family limitation, and growing awareness of the problems posed by 2 or 3 per cent annual growth of population, governments have been willing to encourage, even to enforce, family limitation. India during the 1970s saw the ill-fated attempt of Mrs Ghandi to launch a major programme of vasectomy and in 1980 the Chinese government announced a nationwide attempt to limit the expansion in numbers. Elsewhere, as in Nigeria, family planning clinics have been spreading since the early 1960s. It is now recognized that governments do have the ability to influence the rate of net reproduction by means of family planning programmes. Whereas only one generation ago, total population was treated as an exogenous variable, not amenable to any form of control, it is now regarded by governments of the more populous nations as at least potentially a variable that can be deliberately manipulated.

Table 31 summarizes trends in world population in recent years. Over the period covered by these data, the rate of growth in the global total has remained constant. This is in contrast to earlier

Table 31 *World populations, 1950–77*

Region	Estimated mid-year population (millions)				Annual percentage growth		
	1950	*1965*	*1970*	*1977*	*1950–77*	*1965–77*	*1970–77*
World	2501	3288	3610	4124	1.9	1.9	1.9
Africa	219	309	352	424	2.3	2.7	2.7
North America	166	214	226	242	1.4	1.0	0.9
Latin America	164	247	283	342	2.8	2.7	2.8
Asia	1368	1824	2027	2355	2.3	2.2	2.2
Europe	392	445	459	478	0.7	0.6	0.6
Oceania	12.6	17.5	19.3	22.2	2.1	2.0	2.0
USSR	180	231	243	260	1.4	1.0	1.0

Source: United Nations *Statistical Yearbook, 1978*, p. 8.

decades, when the annual multiplication was accelerating and appeared destined to continue on that course. At least the position has stabilized, not only globally but in all the regions identified in Table 31. Given the evolution of attitudes reviewed in previous paragraphs, it seems highly likely that the rate of growth will henceforth begin to decline, although the change will necessarily take many decades before the effect is readily apparent.

If it is correct that we are now moving towards something approaching a stable population in the world, a situation which might be achieved by the middle of the next century, some important implications follow for the nature of the development process. As we move into the twenty-first century, it seems reasonable to expect that most of the more populous countries will have a reasonably constant total number of inhabitants, with change upwards or downwards being slow by comparison with recent experience. The crucial problems will focus around the nature of acquired skills, knowledge and habits, and the extent to which these are, or are not, conducive to economic development. While this is a matter of concern to all countries, irrespective of the development level achieved, it is of particular relevance for the small number of very populous nations in the Third World – China, India, Pakistan, Bangladesh and Indonesia, which collectively had 1793 million inhabitants in 1977, or 43 per cent of the world's total.

Impulses for development

Previous chapters have reviewed some of the major development impulses which can be associated with the core–periphery model of the world economy. Three impulses relevant for the peripheral nations have been identified:

1 the European colonization of temperate lands;
2 primary exports, of which the non-renewable minerals and fuels have been specially noted;
3 industrialization for export.

We will briefly summarize the situation with respect to each of these impulses.

The close of the nineteenth century more or less coincided with the termination of Europe's colonization of the world's 'empty' temperate lands. Full nationhood had already been achieved in most cases and the groundwork laid for continuing development aided by the controlled inflow of additional migrants. All of these nations initially depended on the export of primary produce. Although this dependence remains in the case of Australia and New Zealand in particular, the United States by contrast has emerged as the world's leading industrial nation. This particular process of economic development was very specific both in its historical and geographical setting.

Primary exports characterized the early development of Sri Lanka, Malaysia, Brazil and many other tropical countries. Although foodstuffs, beverages and agricultural materials for industrial processing remain important export items for many countries, the strength of this impulse has diminished during the last half century or so; substitute materials provide serious competition for natural products (for instance, synthetic rubber); or crops suitable for temperate climates compete with tropical products – sugarbeet with sugarcane, sunflower oil with palm oil and groundnut oil, etc. Indeed, agricultural productivity in the advanced temperate nations has risen so quickly in recent years that Third World nations are hard put to it to be competitive. At the present time, the most striking impulses for export development lie in minerals and fuels, with petroleum as the single most important item. The total number of countries for which the export of minerals and/or fuels is an important feature of their development is quite large, running to several tens in total. However, in population terms they are all quite small, with only Iran and Nigeria exceeding 30 million inhabitants.

The third group of countries is that which has embarked on export-led industrialization. This is a relatively small group of countries, none of which can be described as 'large' in terms of population. Taiwan and South Korea are two of the larger nations, with respectively 15.5 million and 37 million inhabitants in 1978. Mexico, a country for which industrialization is very important but not quite so dominant as for the other two, had a population of 66.9 million in the same year, and no other country in this group exceeds that population. Indeed, Singapore and Hong Kong are far smaller, while the Philippines stood at 46.4 million in 1978. The achievement of these countries has been remarkable. The scope for them to continue on their chosen paths, and for others to join them, is, unfortunately, limited by the size of the export market that can be opened up. This in turn depends on the willingness of other countries to import manufactures, in particular, the willingness of the advanced industrial nations of the core. Past events demonstrate, and *a priori* reasoning suggests, that the willingness of core nations to import manufactures from the periphery is limited – limited by the actual or potential threat of their own employment. Although it seems reasonable to expect that industrial exports from Mexico, Taiwan and South Korea, for example, will continue to grow rapidly, it would not be reasonable to expect that sufficient markets could be found for the number of states engaging in export-led industrial development to double or treble in the foreseeable future. In particular, it is hard to envisage markets adequate to permit any of the very large states to follow this course.

This leaves a very substantial portion of the world's inhabitants living in countries where the impulse to development originating from external economic demands has so far proved inadequate. Broadly speaking, two categories may be recognized. First is the group of very large nations – China, India, etc. – for which a sufficiently large external stimulus would require such massive resources that it is beyond reasonable expectation. The second category is much smaller in total population but with a fairly high over-all density, and lacking an export resource of sufficient importance to trigger rapid national growth. There may, in addition, have been a history of civil war or conflict with neighbours. Vietnam, Uganda and Ethiopia are examples.

Agriculture as the basis for development

For the group of countries which we have just identified, the agricultural sector must, virtually by definition, be the basis for growth and betterment. However, opinions have differed regarding the best means for achieving this end. In the early post-war period, the problem was perceived very largely in terms of surplus rural population that should be absorbed into manufacturing. Only in this way, so it was thought, could the marginal productivity of labour in agriculture be raised. Experience has led to serious questioning of this doctrine. Capital costs per job in manufacturing are high, which puts severe pressure on limited investment resources. Furthermore, the total number of workers for whom jobs can be usefully created is limited by the small size of the domestic market, which in turn is due to low incomes among the mass of the rural inhabitants. Thus, it is now more generally recognized that direct action to improve agricultural productivity is necessary, backed by investment in rural infrastructure (such as roads) and in the manufacturing industries which produce farm inputs such as fertilizers, pumps and tractors. Water control may also require major investment projects, for the storage and distribution of the precious fluid.

The magnitude of the problem facing the larger countries is indicated by the great contribution which the agricultural sector makes to the Gross Domestic Product: 31 per cent in the case of Pakistan and Indonesia, 36 per cent in India and 54 per cent in Bangladesh. Since productivity in the agricultural sector in these countries is substantially less than in manufacturing and commercial occupations, the proportion of the population engaged in farming pursuits is substantially greater than the share of GDP. As Onyemelukwe (1974) persuasively argues, development under these circumstances must be essentially an indigenous affair. Of course modern science and technology will be needed (and associated advisers), and also a certain amount of large-scale investment, but the key to success will lie in engaging the energies of the masses. For this to be possible, technology must be adapted to the local environmental, economic and social conditions to the greatest extent possible; Onyemelukwe uses the term 'indigenous technology' where others prefer 'appropriate technology'.

This approach does not imply severing economic links with the rest of the world, especially the nations of the core. This is a course of action advocated by the school of thought associated with authors such as Frank (1964, 1966 and 1967) and Furtado (1964); it has spawned the inelegant term 'delinking' (Fishlow *et al.*, 1978). As we have already seen, the fear that these economic links necessarily promote the interests of the core against the periphery is without solid foundation (ch. 3). It will be essential to maintain and foster trade and other connections so that the Third World countries we are considering can *selectively* acquire the capital goods and the skills which, currently, are not available indigenously. But, unlike many other countries which have responded to external stimuli, China, India, and similar countries will have to rely very largely upon development processes that are endogenous in origin.

Two approaches may be distinguished, which for convenience can be termed 'big push' and 'incremental' strategies. In the imagery of Rostow's 'take off' into self-sustained growth, one can visualize the need for a massing of effort to achieve a critical point, beyond which the path of growth is fundamentally different from that which led to the take off. Onyemelukwe (1974) takes this view, as does Mabogunje (1980b). A qualitative change is envisaged which, it is argued, can only be obtained through some mechanism of radical transformation.

In the period following the last world war it was widely believed that land reform would provide the requisite big push. Land reform can mean many different things and may be undertaken for a variety of purposes. The general feature is the redistribution of rights in land but there is immense variation in the practical implementation. At one level, as in parts of India, reform meant little more than the conversion of insecure tenancy into more stable tenancy or ownership rights. In Iran, Mexico and elsewhere, large estates were expropriated and sub-divided. The degree of equality achieved has also varied. Bangladesh is a country with a remarkably equal distribution of land among those who are fortunate enough to be farmers. Throughout much of Latin America and parts of India, the main beneficiaries have been the more 'progressive', middle-sized farmers. Results of land reform programmes have been mixed, both in terms of economic efficiency (higher output) and social equality. Indeed, as Warriner (1969) notes, in some cases output actually falls. Two features of the accumulated experience deserve particular notice. First, to be successful, a structural transformation of one element in the production system requires complementary changes, whether in the provision of credit, marketing arrangements, water control or farm advisory facilities. In other words, some form of 'package' is necessary if a radical and rapid change is to occur (Lehmann, 1974; Pearse, 1980). Second, great care must be exercised lest those whose interests are threatened by the change –

usually the owners of large estates and suppliers of traditional credit, but also perhaps the town-based political élite – subvert the reforms in any one of the many ways that are available. Some landlords in India have circumvented legislation to protect tenants by calling them 'servants', whereby their security is less than before the legislation was passed.

With these problems in mind, Mabogunje (1980b) insists that nothing short of a complete transformation of the rural settlement and landownership system will suffice, analogous to the restructuring of the agrarian landscape that occurred in Scandinavia and England in the late eighteenth and early nineteenth centuries. The essence of the argument is that, because man is a social creature, the behaviour of individuals is conditioned by the prevailing norms. Particularly in the poorer and more traditional societies, should an individual change his own pattern of behaviour in any way he will be forced back into the traditional pattern by the strength of the group mores. On this basis, so it is argued, piecemeal changes can have little impact, since cumulative development is prevented by the ossifying effects of custom. On this premise, and in the light of historical and contemporary experience, Mabogunje concludes that the 'big push' approach is essential. It is visualized that only by 'unfreezing' all the relevant economic and social impediments to development simultaneously, by creating a new (and better) structure and then 'freezing' this, will rapid and sustained development become possible.

While it would be difficult to deny that on occasions a 'big push' approach is right, there are at least four reasons for scepticism regarding the *general* applicability of this approach. The empirical evidence marshalled by Mabogunje relates to five major reorganizations: Parliamentary Enclosure in England; the transfer of land from the public domain into private ownership in the United States from 1785 onwards; Russia's post-1917 creation of collective and state farms; the push to create cooperatives in China from 1955 onwards; and Tanzania's villagization programme that dates from 1962. England's enclosure movement depended on the application by a sufficient number of proprietors in a parish for an Enclosure Award (in some cases the 'sufficiency' of proprietors was a single landowner). In other words, the benefits of enclosure had to be perceived prior to any action being taken, which implies that the incremental changes which had previously been proceeding had exhausted the capabilities of the old open-field system. In this case, incremental change – knowledge of crop rotations and livestock management in particular – could no longer be accommodated in the old structure. While it is certainly true that post-enclosure improvement was rapid and sustained, this improvement could not have occurred in the absence of farmers' awareness of the opportunities. A rather similar interpretation of the opening of the public domain in America seems to be warranted. As for Russia and China, the former's organization of agriculture was as much concerned with the extraction of surplus from the countryside for industrial investment as it was with raising farm output, while cooperatives in China built upon the traditional structure of farming organized around the control of water supplies. In any case, one may doubt whether Russia has in fact been as successful with her agriculture as she might have been if less Draconian measures had been employed. Finally, recent reports indicate that the *ujamaa* villages of Tanzania have proved to be an embarrassing failure, owing to the lack of provision of the basic facilities (schools, clinics, water supplies, etc.) that were intended to offset the disadvantages of greater distances to the croplands.

The second reason for scepticism about the 'big push' approach is the danger of a serious reaction. Until recently, it appeared that Iran was being relatively successful in modernizing at a rapid pace. In addition to the extraordinary expenditure on armaments, large-scale irrigation and power projects were implemented, roads and other infrastructure built, and many other fundamental changes put in hand, including the emancipation of women. The toppling of the Shah and the reassertion of fundamentalist Muslim orthodoxy probably has much less to do with the corruption and brutality which undoubtedly existed in Iran than the fact that change was happening too quickly, cutting too fundamentally at the foundations of vested interests.

Bangladesh, Indonesia (Java), much of India and much of China are already so densely populated, with enormous numbers of very small farms, that a *drastic* reorganization of the farming and settlement system is probably impossible and almost certainly undesirable. Two crucial needs stand out. First is the need for adequate water control. Prior to the Meiji restoration in Japan, a great deal had been done to rationalize irrigation systems within catchments, thereby raising yields and paving the way for subsequent agricultural improvements. Java and China likewise have long-established and sophisticated irrigation systems, which nevertheless can still be improved. For India, the Punjab irrigation development in the nineteenth century and tube wells in the twentieth, both provided a major impetus for change. The second need is to find ways of raising productivity within traditional farming systems, not only by better water control but also by the introduction of new plant varieties and associated husbandry practices, such as fertilization and weed control.

Scepticism also arises for a fourth reason. To argue that innovation is prevented by the pressure to conform is to deny that any significant changes have occurred in the past. Such a denial is contrary to the available evidence. Many of the staple food crops of Africa are exotics – maize and cassava being two notable cases. Indigenous farmers created the cocoa and groundnut export trades of West Africa, the rice export trade of Burma depended on indigenous colonization and rubber small-holders are important in Malaysia. The so-called 'green revolution' has had remarkably wide acceptance in India and elsewhere (Pearse, 1980), though providing plenty of problems as well as successes. Altogether, the argument that social imperatives prevent *any* change cannot, in the light of experience all over the world, be sustained.

On the other hand, the case adduced by Mabogunje can properly be used in considering whether the rate of change is fast enough, and its character appropriate, for what is 'necessary' in the given circumstances. There can be no dispute but that in all the more populous less developed nations there are powerful vested interests whose prime concern is either to prevent change that is beneficial to the masses, or to subvert it, in order to maintain and enhance their own wealth and power. It is equally true that tribal, caste and ethnic differences may make it very difficult to obtain the necessary cooperation of the whole nation for the development that is needed. The essentially tribal conflict between the supporters of Mr R. Mugabe, Prime Minister of Zimbabwe, and of Mr J. Nkomo is a sad feature of post-independence politics that was evident during the independence struggle and even before, and is a theme with many variations all over the world.

This leads to a very obvious, but nevertheless fundamental, observation. Whether one is a proponent of the 'big push' thesis or, as the present author, prefers a more incremental approach, it is manifest that for any policy to be successful and yield tangible results, it must be tailored to the local conditions. This is implicit in the five examples selected by Mabogunje: each case provides a different solution, geared to the manifestly different conditions of time and place. Nobody would suggest that the principles of Parliamentary Enclosure are appropriate for China, although it may be the case that Chinese experience with cooperatives could be helpful in the context of Tanzania.

The history and social structure of China is very different from that of Indonesia (Java), and both differ from the nations of the Indian sub-continent, which in turn differ from each other. There are equally striking variations within states. The three main tribal groups of Nigeria are remarkably different. The Ibo of the east had, by the 1970s, achieved a pervasive presence throughout Nigeria as clerks and mechanics, in the Army and the Civil Service. Through their eagerness for education and zeal of application in trades of various kinds, many Ibos had been able to leave their seriously over-populated homeland – and in so doing provided serious and unwelcome competition for the Yoruba and Hausa peoples. This situation provides an important part of the background of their abortive attempt in the 1960s to secede, claiming in justification the right to control the profits of 'their' oil. The greater part of the oil industry at the time happened to be located in Ibo territory, or on the lands of kindred people, in the vicinity of Port Harcourt.

Prior to the civil war, the Nigerian Tobacco Corporation was active in promoting the cultivation of tobacco and thereby was providing a far better service to the ordinary farmers than the official agricultural advisory service. In the then Western Region, the first step in identifying new tobacco cropland was a desk exercise based on topographic, soil and climatic data. An officer of the Corporation would then inspect the likely areas and identify villages that *prima facie* were suitable. Either he or a colleague would then visit the village Chief to talk about tobacco and its cultivation, in quite general terms. Some six months later, there would be a further visit. If the Chief expressed interest, a detailed proposal would be discussed: the area of land to be set aside annually for tobacco, the Corporation to supply seed and oversee the cultivation, etc. If the Chief approved and subsequently gained the assent of his village, a third meeting with a Corporation official could clinch the deal. Once the cultivation of tobacco had started, with appropriate safeguards against pests and diseases, and a carefully specified programme of cultivation and fertilization established, it was very common for the villagers to become curious as to whether similar novelties would be beneficial for their traditional crops, which were mainly subsistence foodstuffs (yams, cassava, millet, maize, etc.). West of Ibadan in the mid 1960s the improvement being wrought in the villages that had elected to grow tobacco was striking.

This is but one instance, drawn from my personal experience, of a development process closely tuned to the local social and economic conditions. Whether a similar approach would be equally successful in other societies is not a matter for assertion but is something that warrants careful empirical study. There is a very substantial literature on village-level development in India, which provides much insight into the need for a sensitive understanding of the society in question. While it would clearly be wrong to say that foreigners cannot acquire this understanding, the sheer scale of the enterprise requires an essentially indigenous effort.

The question of culture

To recapitulate very briefly, the argument in relation to the major less developed nations (China, India, etc.) is as follows. Given the scale of the development which is needed, it is manifest that the main impulse must be derived from internal sources. Furthermore, the major priority must be to raise purchasing power in the rural sector, which implies an increase in productivity in farming. This in turn implies a widespread pattern of change which touches many sensitive points in the economic and social structure. For a development strategy to be successful it must be tailored to the specific context. Therefore, the development process can be expected to vary from one nation to another, and even within nations. By the logic of experience, we are driven to examine a problem that has for several decades been unfashionable in the development literature, wedded as we have been to the concept that western ways could be exported all over the world. In abandoning this proposition, we cannot avoid the question whether cultural differences may have a bearing on the rate and nature of development. At the risk of being labelled 'racist', it is to this problem that we now turn. In doing so, it is useful to cast our minds back over the last 150 years or thereabouts, for attitudes to the cultural variable have changed remarkably. For our purpose, it is useful to identify two separate streams of thought, both of which have been influential in their time but now are less highly regarded, with a view to seeing what we can learn that may be relevant to the present day. The first of these themes we may label the genetic, and the other the religious, explanation of economic development.

Charles Darwin published his *On the Origin of Species by Means of Natural Selection* in 1859, in which he set forth the arguments for evolution by natural variation and selection – the 'survival of the fittest'. Six years later, the Bohemian monk G. J. Mendel made available to the world the results of his painstaking work with the common garden pea. Unlike Darwin's treatise, the labours of Mendel were neglected for some decades and it was Galton (1883) who really founded the eugenics movement, which subsequently gained scientific respectability from the rediscovery of Mendel's laws and the development of genetics as a science from about 1900 onwards. The combination of Darwinian selection and Mendelian inheritance created an exciting new arena in which the scientific investigation of racial characteristics could be contemplated. Although it was not until the 1930s that the genetic basis of inheritance was reasonably well understood, the temptation to speculate on the possible connection between 'race' and economic development proved irresistible.

The way in which attitudes changed has been succinctly described by Huntington (1927, p. 1):

A century or two ago it was widely held that all races and even all individuals are equally endowed by nature. Physically there might indeed be enormous diversity, but differences in character and mentality were supposed to be due entirely to training. Then there arose a school of thinkers who violently combated this idea. They wrote books like *The Inequality of Races*, by Gobineau, in order to convince the world that mentally as well as physically one race actually differs from another. The theory of evolution reinforced their conclusions; according to that theory it is almost inevitable not only that different races should be in different stages of mental as well as physcial development, but that they should develop along different and divergent lines. Then came Mendel with his explanation of the mechanism by which individual traits are passed from parent to child, and Galton with his insistence on the importance of heredity. At last the idea of racial differences became so firmly established that a leading scientist could say: 'Race has played a far larger part than either language or nationality in moulding the destinies of man.'

Although Huntington was scrupulous in regarding genetic inheritance as an hypothesis to be examined, with the passage of time his conviction regarding its relevance became stronger rather than weaker (see Huntington, 1945 and Martin, 1973). Similar views were held by Toynbee (vol. 1, 1934). He conceived of history as the unfolding of a drama which, in terms of a mythological formulation, could be conceived as the interplay of two superhuman forces which he identified as 'race' and 'environment'.

From the mid nineteenth century onwards our knowledge of the world's geography was becoming sufficiently good for scholars to attempt not only systematic description but also explanation of observed patterns. Although by no means the first, one of the more influential scholars in this field was Ratzel, whose *Anthropogeographie*, published in two parts, appeared in 1882 and 1889. One of the fields for speculation was the connection, if any, between conditions of the natural environment and the characteristics of society and economy. Early in the twentieth century, one of the more dogmatic environmental treatises was published by Semple (1911), and, as we have already seen (p. 35), notions of environmental determinism were widespread in both the nineteenth and early to mid twentieth centuries. On the then available evidence, there seemed to be a close connection between the distribution of 'civilization' and the temperate latitudes, a notion taken to its extreme by Markham as late as 1942. The more generally accepted moderate version of this doctrine is reflected in the thought of Marshall (1890). He devoted a chapter to the health and strength of the population, taking it as self-evident that a high level of vigour was necessary for national economic success, and: 'Vigour depends partly on race qualities: but these, so far as they can be explained at all, seem to be chiefly due to climate' (Marshall, 1949 edn, p. 195).

Although the environmental hypothesis for explaining the wide variations in the human condition can be traced back to the Greeks (Glacken, 1967), there was undoubtedly a great increase of interest in this idea toward the end of the nineteenth century. Whether it was coincidental that this idea surfaced at about the same time as concepts of genetic inheritance were being elaborated is a moot point. That in the hands of some authors both were grossly overstated is not in doubt; nor is there any doubt that the concept of genetic inheritance and environmental control came to be closely intertwined the one with the other. Were either hypothesis to be true, then all the world outside the temperate zones settled by people of European stock would be condemned to the role of hewers of wood and drawers of water. The general validity of both hypotheses was in any case disputed and denied. Even the modified version, which identified a link from environment through disease to human energy and economic attainment, became increasingly suspect as medical science progressed. Certainly by the end of the second world war, it was apparent that the nutritional and disease problems of the tropical and equatorial zones could be mastered. For example, DDT had a spectacular effect in eradicating malaria not only in Italy and other Mediterranean countries but also in India, Sri Lanka and elsewhere. The fact that the malarial mosquito has made a come-back should not obscure the immense optimism of the 1950s.

At this time, western industrial civilization apparently was available neatly packaged for export, the export drive led by hosts of advisers who were mostly European or American. Any notion that the standard package might not suit all customers was dismissed – as much by the would-be recipients as by the willing sellers. To admit that the standard formula might be inappropriate was to suggest that countries do not necessarily follow the same path of development and that such divergences might arise from either or both of two causes: the condition of the physical environment; or cultural differences. The former possibility has proved reasonably easy to accept, since it is readily apparent in the agricultural sector. It is now generally accepted that crops and livestock do have to be bred for specific environmental conditions, and that husbandry techniques must be adapted to the local conditions of climate, soil, terrain and water regime.

At first sight it would seem likely that industrial technology can be much more standard throughout a wide range of environmental and cultural circumstances than is the case for agriculture. That this is not necessarily so is shown by the papers and discussion of a conference held by the International Economic Association on the problem of 'appropriate' technology in the development of Third World countries (Robinson, 1979). The bibliographies associated with the papers bear witness to the amount of interest which has attached to this problem ever since the seminal but highly theoretical work of Sen (1960). Running through the proceedings of the conference are several themes of major importance. Over a wide range of manufacturing, there is not one single production-function but a large range of feasible functions. Given the immense variation in factor endowments from one country to another, one of the major tasks is to adapt manufacturing technology to achieve the most economical production. A necessary condition is to ensure that the relative prices of the factors reflect their scarcity/abundance, and to ensure that the currency is realistically valued. All too often, capital is made artificially cheap, which encourages capital-intensive production, whereas it is usually advantageous to economize on capital and use either or both labour and natural resources intensively – a policy followed in Taiwan with notable success. This assumes, of course, that the end product is known, i.e. that a 'western' commodity is appropriate. However, the very nature of the product and the way it is marketed may be a matter for careful enquiry in the light of local habits. Therefore, both in the decision regarding what to produce and how to produce it, careful adaptation to local cultural circumstances is essential. The conference identified the urgent need for explicit research on both fronts, and the idea was mooted of some form of international clearing system so that developing countries can draw on the stock of knowledge that is relevant for them. The concept espoused by Rostow, Kuznets and others, of science as a common stock of knowledge, available to all mankind, is therefore seen in a highly qualified light. Even though the basic principles of science are generally available, they must be applied to local circumstances as determined by environmental and cultural conditions. This being so, there is no necessary reason why the path of development should be identical in all cultures. Also the necessity for research and development in order to generate appropriate technologies implies that economic development may not occur at the same tempo in all cultural areas. In short, the plea for 'appropriate' technology must be interpreted as a plea for account to be taken of cultural as well as economic differences.

This brings us to the second of the themes identified earlier in this chapter. Early in the present century, Max Weber published several studies of world religions, of which *The Protestant Ethic and the Spirit of Capitalism* is the best known (Weber, 1976). In this study, Weber asks the question: to what extent did the key characteristics of the Protestant, and more particularly Calvinist, ethic help to create the capitalist economy of Western Europe and North America? At the time Weber wrote, it seemed self-evident that the modern industrial economy could be equated with 'capitalism', and it was with capitalism that Weber was exclusively concerned. At the turn of the century, the dominance of 'European' economic power was such that it also seemed self-evident that Europe, rather than China or India or anywhere else, must have possessed some unique characteristic not found elsewhere. Weber identified this as economic rationalism, manifest in the capitalists' drive to accumulate and the concept of labour as a divine calling, both traits associated with the Protestant ethic. The proposition certainly has an element of persuasiveness, though Weber himself signally fails to provide any rigorous test of the hypothesis. The difficulty of so doing is manifest in Tawney's (1926) treatment of the same general theme.

Less interested in the 'essence' of events and structures, Tawney draws attention to the turbulent economic changes that preceded the Reformation and which in part called into existence the very religion which facilitated the further development of science, commerce and economy to pave the way for the industrial development which, in the nineteenth century, was pre-eminently capitalist in nature. For Tawney, the revolution associated with the Reformation was the release of the *individual* from the trammels of traditional hierarchical social and economic organizations sanctified by religion. Under the new dispensation, individual effort and gain were blessed. As a result, energies were mobilized on a scale and in a manner that was without precedent. This view has close parallels with the interpretation offered by List as long ago as 1841, that prosperity is a direct function of the liberties enjoyed by individuals.

However the detail may be interpreted, there is little doubt that the industrial revolution of the eighteenth and nineteenth centuries did in fact depend in large measure upon the relatively unconstrained initiative of many individuals, who between them created a new economic order. Given the circumstances of time and place, it is relatively easy to explain why the modern world economy required a particular set of cultural characteristics. The fact that Europe had these characteristics is an important part of the explanation for the birth of the modern order there rather than elsewhere.

We must remember, though, that this particular tradition arose at a time when the economy spawned by Western Europe and its offshoots overseas dominated the world. At the time Tawney wrote, Japan was still remote and apparently of little significance; the revolution in Russia had yet to prove its ability to transform the economy of that large and sprawling giant. Weber is rather explicit in supposing that the Protestant ethic was a *necessary* condition for 'capitalist' (i.e. modern) development. Tawney is much more careful, though in the context of his time the same inference could easily be read into his work. Clearly, any such inference implies that modern technology and associated economic development cannot readily be transplanted into other cultures. Since this proposition became unacceptable, especially after the second world war, the Weber/Tawney analysis has fallen out of fashion. Indeed, it was assumed that the relevant attributes of western economic man could be exported along with the technology. This assumption, in turn, has been found wanting: too often, aid administrators, economic advisers and government officials have bemoaned the 'perverse' behaviour of peasants and other producers.

The historical fact that the modern world economy was created by Europeans and that this creation was associated with Protestantism cannot be denied. However, we cannot assume that economic development must necessarily be in the European image the world over. Furthermore, we must entertain two possibilities:

1 some cultures may be more receptive to modern, science-based methods than others. Note that this does not necessarily imply a 'capitalist' way of doing things;
2 one or more cultures may be more adept at exploiting the new opportunities than the culture of their origin.

In other words, we must at least ask the question whether the present position and future prospects of nations might be influenced, at least in part, by cultural differences. At the present time, this is a comparatively unfashionable topic and in any case is one that is not amenable to rigorous 'scientific' analysis. Nevertheless, some comment and speculation is called for, if only in the light of the case which some scholars advance for a 'big push' in order to break existing socio-economic constraints (p. 150) and the evidence for a multiplicity of production-functions which relate to wide variations in circumstances (p. 158).

A rather extreme view of the importance of culture has been taken by Kahn (1979), who regards the inheritors of neo-Confucian civilization as the countries best equipped to 'catch up' with the core countries. His 'heroes' of modern development are Japan, South Korea and Taiwan, with Singapore and Hong Kong as also notably successful but much smaller. In summary:

We believe that both aspects of the Confucian ethic – the creation of dedicated, motivated, responsible, and educated individuals and the enhanced sense of commitment, organizational identity, and loyalty to various institutions – will result in all the neo-Confucian societies having at least potentially higher growth rates than other cultures. (Kahn, 1979, p. 122)

Whether it is the Confucian ethic itself which is crucial, or other characteristics of the Asiatic societies, must be regarded as a moot point. After all, there is a very long tradition of technological development, especially in China and Japan. Many Chinese innovations were adopted in Europe, materially contributing to the developments which led up to the industrial revolution. Between *c*. 1150 and 1757, the list of such transfers is long, including gunpowder, the compass, paper manufacture, printing and numerous mechanical devices (Singer, *et al.*, 1956, pp. 770–2). Likewise, many of Japan's present-day firms grew out of businesses which for generations had been making guns or other mechanical/metal goods (Ishikawa, 1979). Indeed, a visit to any major museum will quickly convince the sceptic that Japan had superb craftsmen before the Meiji Restoration, working in a wide variety of materials. Closely associated with these characteristics is the long tradition of organized government and all that this implies in terms of social discipline. The following passage captures something of the significance of this long tradition, and indicates just how widely the consequences ramify:

China developed what is perhaps the oldest system of roads for everyday use, with post-stages comparable with the magnificent organization of the Incas in later times. Even before the Chow dynasty (*c*. 1100–255 BC), communications were controlled and roads maintained by a highways commissioner. During the Chow dynasty the traffic necessitated the prescription of a uniform scale of size for wheeled vehicles, prohibition of furious driving, and traffic regulations at crowded crossings. Roads were classified into five grades: (a) pathways for men and pack-animals; (b) roads taking a vehicle of narrow gauge; (c) roads with room for a wider wagon; (d) roads wide enough for wagons to pass one another; (e) highroads taking three wagons abreast. (Singer *et al.*, 1954, pp. 713–4.)

This long tradition of technological sophistication and bureaucratic organization is not confined to China and Japan. Until annexed by the Japanese in 1910, Korea had enjoyed 2000 years of continuous independent history as an organized kingdom. Even Indonesia, which experienced the longest colonial domination of any major peoples, has an indigenous civilization that makes the Dutch ascendancy a rather short episode. And so we could multiply the examples. The essential point is that the whole of the South-East Asia culture realm has a deeply ingrained tradition of national political and administrative integration which is an important requisite for rapid development in the latter part of the twentieth century.

Conclusion

The argument of this chapter may be summarized quite briefly. For an important group of nations with large populations, exogenous influences are unlikely to be dominant in the development process and reliance must be placed on endogenous processes. This implies the adaptation of technology and organizational forms to suit the local conditions of physical environment and social structure. Such adaptation means that ready-made answers are not available from the stock of common scientific knowledge, at least, not without suitable modifications. To the extent that, in the late twentieth and twenty-first centuries, the drive for modernization in the larger countries must come from within societies, rather than from outside, the nature of the societies themselves becomes the prime focus of attention. In this respect, it would appear that the countries of Asia – China, Japan, Indonesia, India, etc. – have some important advantages relative to many other nations, in the length of their histories and the sophistication of their civilizations. However, this is a field for speculative inquiry rather than dogmatic assertion: it is a field which had become unfashionable, almost taboo, until quite recently.

The 'big push' approach appears to be inherently implausible as a solution for the very large less advanced nations. China's 'cultural leap' has not produced the results that were expected, and other attempts at contrived revolutionary change have been equally partial in their success. Viewed over the long term, incremental change has been more important. Such change leads to a position where some radical restructuring may be necessary in order to accommodate further incremental evolution. On this view, the ability of nations to respond to their opportunities cannot be divorced from their history over the past centuries, even millennia.

6   Environmental change

Ever since Malthus and Ricardo, all discussions of the pressure on food supplies have started from the assumption that population is the active factor and Nature the fixed. (Utterström, 1955, p. 3)

The concept of a stable Holocene environment is quite untenable. (Goudie, 1977, p. 95)

Recent decades have witnessed a dramatic change of view concerning the constancy or otherwise of important components of the natural environment. According to the old orthodoxy, the natural conditions – especially of climate – could be taken as invariant during the historical period, except in so far as man himself had intervened and effected changes, as with forest clearance and the drainage of swamps. While it would be premature to say that a new orthodoxy has emerged, complete with an adequate chronology of changes, yet there is now sufficient evidence to show that substantial changes of climate and sea level have occurred within the comparatively recent past to justify the proposition that, in taking an historical view, serious consideration must be given to the possibility that environmental change has occurred sufficient to affect the course of history. In this chapter we will explore some aspects of these changing ideas, and in particular the relevance of environmental change to economic conditions, both in the past and prospectively in the future.

The time-span with which we must now concern ourselves is substantially greater than has been relevant hitherto, except in the last chapter. As will become apparent, the geographical scope of inquiry is also large; changes in sea level have a world-wide impact; climatic change is one region is generally associated with complementary changes elsewhere, as part of the global atmospheric circulation system. As a result, we are, in terms of Figure 4 (see page 24), located in the upper and right hand corner of the plane defined by the a and b axes. One of the factors which is potentially relevant for the explanation of long-period economic phenomena is change of climate, or other aspects of the physical environment, arising independently of man's actions. Therefore, one purpose of the present chapter is to reinforce the point that as the time-scale of study varies so must we be willing to re-examine our assumptions concerning causation. In addition, historical events throw some light on a contemporary problem, whether and to what extent the world's climate is being changed by the heat released through the combustion of coal, oil and gas, through an increase in the atmosphere's CO_2 content, and in other ways. These anxieties are usually expressed in global terms, without reference to the potential for man-induced climatic change to have substantially greater effects in some areas than others.

The old orthodoxy: the constant environment

Our forefathers were aware that climate does change. Efforts were made to organize official observation networks, partly with the intention of monitoring these changes, as early as the 1770s in France and 1821 in Prussia (Lamb, 1966, p. 2). Interest in the subject is evident in a discussion held at the Royal Meteorological Society in 1911. Nevertheless, the more general view in the nineteenth century was that climate had remained constant. It was only when the warming which occurred from the 1890s to the 1940s had become obvious to all – as the period was drawing to its close – that general interest in the topic revived.

This development of interest can also be linked to changing ideas about the origin of the earth. While the concept of a Creation dominated religious and lay thinking, it was widely believed that the Earth came into existence, more or less in its present configuration, some 6000 years ago. Such changes as did occur in the surface features were ascribed to catastrophic events. Only at the end of the eighteenth century and early in the nineteenth did the work of men like Hutton and Playfair begin the revolution in ideas which led to the realization that the world has a geological history. That the Earth has been in existence for as long as 4600 million years has become evident only very recently. For a long time, as awareness of geological history became more clearly defined, it was believed that the significant changes had occurred prior to the historical epoch. By the end of the nineteenth century, the four main phases of the Alpine glaciation had been recognized. Nevertheless: 'It is not many years since it was generally believed that variations of climate came to an end with the Quaternary Ice Age, a period moreover which was placed hundreds of thousands of years ago' (Brooks, 1949, p. 281).

Notwithstanding major publications by Brooks in particular (1925 and 1926; the latter was revised in 1949), by Huntington (1945) and others, the orthodox view of unchanging climate in the historical period dominated the literature of geography and history right into the 1950s and even to the present day. Sauer, writing in 1956 (p. 53) could say:

A priori it is reasonable to consider that the contemporary pattern of climates had become more or less established before the last ice retreat began. Lesser later local climatic oscillations have been found but have been improperly extended and exaggerated, however, in archaeological literature.

The whole tenor of Sauer's essay is to doubt the evidence for climatic change in the historical period and to minimize its significance.

Three books, published within six years of each other, proposed the thesis that the history of mankind is played out on a stage which is unchanging, except as it is affected by man himself (Fairgrieve, 1927; George, 1930; Bryan, 1933). The same theme was repeated by Whittlesey in 1949 in his consideration of European history. Two passages capture the essence of this attitude. First, Whittlesey (1949, p. 2) explains the attractions of geography for an historian:

I had originally planned to follow history as a profession, and had taught it for a year, besides completing a historical dissertation. Geography had come to my attention and stirred my interest while I was at the graduate school, because it built a solid foundation beneath my historical studies.

The second is from George (1930, p. 10):

Arid conditions may have encroached upon lands previously fertile and populous, as in Central Asia. A harbour here and there has silted up; the sea has receded or encroached along a few strips of coast. . . . One or two rivers have changed their course; a few square miles here and there have been desolated by a volcanic eruption or by a landslip. The greatest change of this kind that Europe has witnessed since history began is the conversion of the Zuyder Zee, once an inland lagoon, into an arm of the sea. . . . For historical purposes at least, we are justified in saying that the physical features of the earth undergo no change of which account need be taken.

The essentially episodic and local nature of environmental change is a theme reiterated by Russell in 1956, in the same conference on man's role in changing the face of the earth to which Sauer also contributed.

This 'static' view of the environment was clearly consistent with the idea of local variations due to specific causes. It was also consistent with the existence of cyclical variations about constant mean values, subject to the cycles being of relatively short duration. One of the first periodicities so identified was that of the eleven year sunspot cycle, which, in articles appearing between 1862 and 1877, Jevons called in as an aid to explain the cyclical behaviour of economic activity (see Jevons, 1909). The first classic study of climatic variation was the astonishing compilation of instrumental records, lake level data, harvest dates, etc., published by Brückner in 1890. On the basis of careful examination of these data, Brückner concluded that there is a recurring pattern of hot and cold, dry and wet periods with a recurrence time of about thirty-five or thirty-six years: he found no evidence to suggest longer period or 'permanent' changes of climate. Simpson, writing in 1926 (p. 119), reviewing Brückner's findings in the light of more recent information, came to the conclusion:

There seems little doubt that, while there has been no progressive desiccation or permanent change of climate during the historic period, there have been long periods, much longer than the thirty-five years for a complete Brückner cycle, when the conditions were different from the present – periods of increased rainfall and periods of increased desiccation; but these have been temporary, and the normal conditions have ultimately been restored.

Within a decade, Abel published the first edition (1935) of his classic study of agricultural fluctuation in Europe over a span of seven centuries (see Abel, 1980). Highly dependent on climate as agriculture is, and given the relatively simple technology that prevailed until recently, one might expect long-period environmental variations to be potent in changing supply–demand relationships and hence the prices of produce and prosperity of farmers. Although Abel mentions periods of poor harvests attributable to adverse seasons, it is clear that he regards fluctuations arising from this cause as brief episodes that interrupt broad trends arising from other causes. His influential work is firmly cast in the orthodox mould of a 'static' environment; later historians have generally followed his lead.

Old orthodoxy challenged prematurely

Ellsworth Huntington was the first scholar who devoted a great deal of time and energy to the problem of elucidating climatic change in the historical period to conclude that major, long-term and world-wide variations had indeed occurred. During his travels in Turkey and Central Asia, he observed the evidence of former civilizations in regions now abandoned and too arid to support cities; he recognized former strand-lines above present lake surfaces, he identified alluvial fans where now no competent river runs, and many other indications of formerly more humid conditions in regions now desert or capable of supporting only nomadic tribesmen. *The Pulse of Asia*, published in 1907, is the first major publication to argue the case for climatic change in the historical span. In addition to his own observations in Turkey and Asia, Huntington drew upon the reports of Jefferson and Bowman in particular, as providing evidence for similar changes in the New World. From 1907 onwards, Huntington devoted much energy to this subject and published a very large number of papers and books wholly or partially devoted to the subject (Martin, 1973). Although an immense amount of work could be done collating documentary, archaeological and topographic evidence, Huntington recognized the twofold limitations of this approach:

1 the potential circularity of the argument from the evidence of human activities and the difficulty of distinguishing causes other than climatic change that might give the same results;
2 the inability to determine absolute dates for the topographical evidence of former rivers, higher strand-lines, etc.

Early in the present century, the most promising source of independent evidence to determine the nature and scale of climatic variation appeared to be provided by the variable thickness of tree rings. Huntington was inspired by a paper that appeared in 1907, in which the yellow pine of Arizona had been dated back to 1392. With characteristic energy, he set out to work on the giant redwoods of California (*Sequoia gigantea*), which at that time were being rapidly felled for commercial timber. During field seasons in 1911 and 1912, he and assistants took measurements on 451 tree stumps; of these, seventy-nine were 2000 years old, three were 3000 years old, and one was 3150 years old. Other workers were engaged in similar work with other tree species.

Special care was taken since different trees are stimulated by different conditions, some trees responding mainly to warmth, some to abundant moisture. Hence before interpretation of the growth curves could be made it was necessary to compare tree measurements over the last century with local meteorological records. That work had been done for the yellow pine by A. E. Douglass and for *Sequoia gigantea* by Huntington. (Martin, 1973, p. 108)

Notwithstanding the difficulties, work on tree rings continued (Brooks, 1949) but even today there are immense problems of inferring climatic change from the evidence of annual tree growth (Fritts, 1976). In addition, Huntington, eager to establish world-wide chronologies, made heroic generalizations from the limited data available. An example is his examination of Toynbee's listing of the major migrations of nomads from the deserts and steppes of Asia and Africa. Toynbee considered these migrations to have been due to climatic pulsations. To test this hypothesis, Huntington plotted the dates of the migrations alongside a graph of cyclic variation in tree growth in California (Huntington, 1945, pp. 562–4). Even if tree rings are an adequate measure of climatic change there is no *a priori* reason for supposing that changes in all parts of the world will be simultaneous and in the same direction; indeed, on theoretical grounds one would expect desiccation in one area to be matched by greater humidity elsewhere. The third reason why Huntington's work on climatic change received much less notice than it deserved was its close identification with a view of human affairs that postulated unidirectional causation from the physical environment and genetic inheritance. The concept of environmental determinism, which was given its most dogmatic presentation by Semple in 1911, was very quickly abandoned as untenable. Although a less extreme exponent of this view than Semple, Huntington was tarred with the same brush.

Evidence on climatic change was not confined to tree rings: instrumental evidence has been available for approximately 300 years; dates of grain and grape harvests have been recorded; inland lakes are bounded by higher strand-lines; plant and animal remains are indicative of former climates; and varves (alternating layers of lacustrine sediment) also provide clues. Early in the present century, however, the amount of such information was limited and the major problem of assigning absolute dates had not been solved except in the case of varves, but even in this case later evidence has thrown some varve datings into doubt. Not surprisingly, the sceptics discounted Huntington, just as they also discounted Toynbee (1934–59).

It would be wrong to give the impression that Huntington and Toynbee were the only heterodox scholars in the earlier part of the present century. Brooks (1949) refers to the belief of Brückner that emigration from Europe to the USA depended on rainfall, and also to Peake's study of Aryan migrations, which he attributed to drought. Both authors published these opinions in the first quarter of the present century. Brooks himself could not absolutely resist the temptation to argue in the same vein. In general, though, the basic problem facing the protagonists of environmental change as a significant factor affecting the course of history remained that of establishing a precisely dated chronology. It was only after the second world war that real progress was made towards the solution of this problem.

Towards a new orthodoxy: the changing environment

One of the major milestones on the road to a revised view of environmental change is the 1957 classic work by Charlesworth. Although he devoted most of his attention to the glacial era, one chapter is devoted to questions of climatic and sea-level changes in post-glacial times right up to relatively recent historical times. Despite the wealth of previous literature, Charlesworth could only tentatively assign absolute dates to very few episodes; major advances in this respect had to await the development and application of modern dating techniques, and a great deal of further painstaking examination of documentary and other records. The fruits of these labours are embodied in two volumes published in 1977, which demonstrate beyond any reasonable doubt that environmental change has indeed continued throughout the historical period. While Lamb deals solely with climate, Goudie includes sea-level changes and other environmental variations, though mainly with reference to the long geological span. Both authors are cautious concerning the establishment of general chronologies, scrupulously observing the limitations of the data. Likewise, neither indulges in heroic assumptions about the implications of the identified environmental changes for the prosperity of nations and empires. In this respect, the current approach conforms to the scientific standards maintained by Brooks (1925, 1949), though scientists are now able to work with much better data than was available to him.

It is now generally accepted that north-western Europe experienced a 'little optimum' in the period from AD 750–1300:

From about AD 750 to 1200–1300 there was a period of marked glacial retreat which on the whole appears to have been slightly more marked than has been that of the twentieth century. The trees of this phase, which were eventually destroyed by the cold and glacial advances from around AD 1200 onwards, grew on sites where, in our time, trees have not had time, or the necessary conditions, to grow again. In terms of a more precise date, the medieval documents that are available place the most clement period of this optimum, with its mild winters and dry summers, at AD 1080–1180. At this time, the coast of Iceland was relatively unaffected with ice, compared to later centuries, and settlement... was achieved in now inhospitable parts of Greenland. It is also believed that the relative heat and dryness of the summers, which led to the drying up of some peat bogs, was responsible for the plagues of locusts which in this period spread at times over vast areas, occasionally reaching far to the north. For instance, during the summer of 1195 they reached as far as Hungary and Austria. (Goudie, 1977, pp. 119–20)

This period of benign climate was followed by the 'little ice age', marked by the advance of glaciers and deteriorating conditions on marginal upland farms, some of which had to be abandoned. Lamb (1977) cites evidence for the beginning of this phase in the thirteenth century in the Alps; it was not until after AD 1500 that the same phenomena became evident in Greenland, and even later, in the seventeenth century, in Iceland. There is incontrovertible evidence from Iceland of two farms that were overwhelmed by the advancing ice, one between 1695 and 1709 and the other some time after 1712 (Parry, 1978, p. 168). This period of greater cold in north-western Europe came to an end during the nineteenth century, ushering in the present period of relatively favourable climate in this part of the world.

Goudie offers evidence from elsewhere showing that substantial changes in climatic conditions have occurred. Of the wealth of examples that could be cited, we will be content with the eastward shift of climatic boundaries that has occurred in Australia (Figure 16). The change was sufficiently marked to have a distinct, and adverse, effect on crop and animal husbandry.

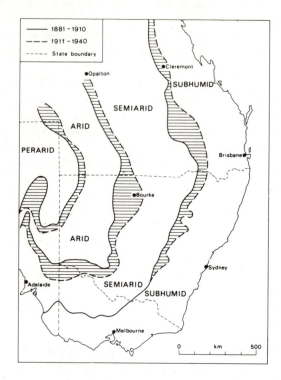

Figure 16   *Shifts in climatic boundaries, eastern Australia, 1881–1910 to 1911–40*
Source: Goudie (1977).

Europe's marginal areas

Although climatic change in particular, and environmental change more generally, cannot be offered as an important general factor in economic affairs and in history, nevertheless in marginal areas it may be of crucial significance. As long ago as 1926, Simpson noted that climatic changes of the duration and magnitude likely to occur in Britain were probably not of great significance; by contrast, in arid regions they would be 'all important'. Virtually the same point was made by Slicher van Bath (1963, pp. 7–8). Reviewing the possibility that climate might be a major factor affecting the course of agrarian history in Europe, he says:

As far as western Europe is concerned this does not seem likely. It would have been so, however, in regions where farming was carried on under conditions of extreme difficulty: Iceland, the north of Scandinavia, the Alps and the tablelands of southern Europe. In northern Europe long, severe winters could be ruinous; a slight drop in the mean annual temperature could make the growing of cereals impossible. Cereal cultivation was given up in Iceland in the late Middle Ages, perhaps on this account. In southern Europe a small decrease in the spring rainfall could endanger the whole grain harvest.

The distinction drawn by Slicher van Bath for the different parts of Europe is confirmed by the present-day pattern of crop-yield variation (Figure 17). From southern England, through the Netherlands, West Germany, East Germany and Poland stretches a belt of low variation in crop yields. Towards northern Europe, the Mediterranean and the Black Sea, variability increases substantially.

Thus, we need not be surprised that it was in respect of two of Europe's marginal areas that scholars were first impressed by the relevance of environmental change, namely, northern Europe and the Mediterranean. Utterström (1955) advanced a powerful case to show that in the history of the Scandinavian countries, Iceland and Greenland, climate has been an important variable. Apart from the evidence which he offered, evidence which subsequently has been criticized (le Roy Ladurie, 1972) but also corroborated, perhaps the most interesting feature of Utterström's paper is the clear fact that changes both of climate and sea level were deeply embedded in the thinking of Scandinavian historians as probable casual factors: citations are numerous and extend back in time to Petterson's 1914 discussion of climatic change as an historical variable. There can be little doubt that the 'little ice age' in northern Europe had disastrous consequences for some areas. In the same issue of the *Scandinavian Economic History Review* as that in which Utterström wrote, Jutikkala examined evidence relating to the proportion of Finland's population that died during the famine of 1696–7. At least one-quarter, and probably in excess of one-third, perished. The famine is attributable to harvest failure due to an excessively cold season following a number of poor harvests occasioned by the same cause. Although the famine was not general to all of what was then

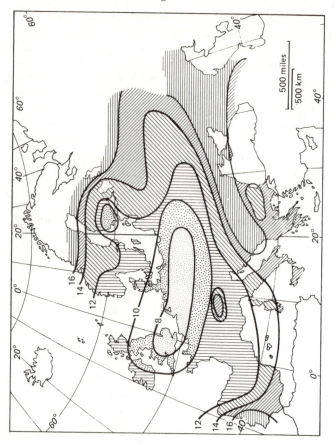

Figure 17 *Variability of crop production in Europe: average precentage departure from normal, 1927–33*

Sweden, it was part of a general climatic deterioration. Reference has already been made to the abandonment of farms in Iceland in the late seventeenth and early eighteenth centuries (p. 171). The decade of the 1690s was known in Scotland as the 'seven ill years'; I personally have clear recollections of Professor Gordon Manley at Bedford College in the 1960s opining that climatic deterioration played a significant part in driving Scotland to the Act of Union in 1707. Finally, Grove (1972), has found unmistakable documentary evidence for the impoverishment of farms in Norway; requests for tax remission and associated evidence of greater landslide, avalanche and flood damage, shows the period 1650–1760 to have been particularly difficult.

To date, the single best study of climatic change and agriculture in northern Europe is that of Parry (1978). He has examined a wealth of documentary, archaeological and other data, in conjunction with the most recent knowledge of the chronology of climatic change. From his careful culling of the data, he is able to identify those areas which have remained continuously suitable for cultivation on climatic grounds over several centuries; and those areas which, at various times, have been brought into use and abandoned. Climate is not the only relevant variable; for example, periods of shortage arising from war will serve to extend the limits of cultivation. However, a reasonably consistent pattern emerges of agriculture extending to higher altitudes during climatically favourable periods and retreating as conditions deteriorate. Using admittedly rather crude criteria and inadequate climatic data, Parry shows that at the present time northern Britain and most of Scandinavia is climatically marginal or sub-marginal for agriculture (Figure 18).

Europe's other major marginal zone has attracted much more attention over the last three decades than the northern lands, at least among English-speaking scholars. The first major landmark is Braudel's (1949) classic study. Given the then exisiting state of knowledge, Braudel could do no more than draw attention to the certainty that significant environmental changes have occurred in the historical period but that in the absence of a precise chronology no firm inferences could be drawn regarding their impact on the course of history. By 1966, Carpenter had thrown caution to the winds – literally, to the movement north and south of the main trade and westerly wind circulations – in an attempt to explain a puzzling discontinuity in Greek civilization, in the thirteenth to eleventh centuries BC. Although his thesis is open to criticism, Carpenter displays a commendable awareness of the interaction of changes in general circulation and topography, and hence the locally differentiated impact of variation.

This is a theme developed by Bryson and Murray (1977) in respect of Mycenae – the same discontinuity that attracted Carpenter's attention. However, these authors also attempt to reconstruct the fluctuation of the track of the westerly airstream in the northern hemisphere over the last millennium, a bold and probably premature attempt. With respect to the Mediterranean and Middle East,

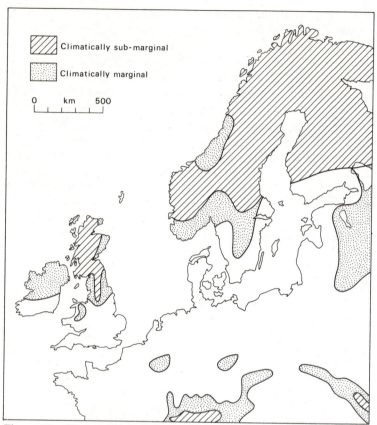

Figure 18   *Climatically marginal land in northern Europe*
Source: Parry (1978).

Butzer (1970) and Wright (1977) among others have examined the
evidence for the immediately post-glacial period and show just how
dramatic the vegetational changes were in response to climatic
variation. However, as is evident from Al-Sayari and Zötl (1978)
and Brice (1978), it is still very difficult to establish what may have
happened, and the significance thereof, during more recent times,
say the last two millennia.

Contemporary interest in climatic change

Three separate sets of events have awakened concern about the
possibility of climatic change and the potential impact on the world

as a whole and the major regions. The three sets of events are: the accumulation of atmospheric carbon dioxide; the large number of extreme climatic events since 1960; and environmental degradation around the margins of deserts.

It has been observed that the amount of carbon dioxide in the atmosphere has been rising for many decades and, if the present trend continues, it is possible that by the middle of the next century the concentration will have become double that of the 1970s. It is common to ascribe this rising concentration of atmospheric CO_2 to the burning of fossil fuels – coal, oil and gas – the world-wide consumption of which has been rising continuously and rapidly. However, it appears that the spread of modern farming techniques and the development of new agricultural methods serves to reduce the amount of humus in the soil, thereby releasing organic carbon into the atmosphere as CO_2. The volume of carbon so released is approximately the same as the volume emitted from the combustion of fuels (Hare, 1980). Furthermore, the world's oceans contain approximately ten times as much carbon as the atmosphere and we do not know much about the exchange processes between air and water. Consequently, there must be doubt whether the observed increase in atmospheric CO_2 will in fact continue, though it is clear that indeed this is a serious possibility.

Atmospheric carbon dioxide is important, among other things, for the way it traps short-wave (infra-red) radiation from the surface of the earth – the so-called greenhouse effect. One may infer that an increase in the CO_2 concentration will enhance this effect, so raising the average temperature of the earth's gaseous mantle. Now it may be that this effect will be counterbalanced by other factors, such as greater reflection of the incoming insolation on account of the rising dust content of the atmosphere. The uncertainties surrounding this whole question are legion and the easy option is to conclude that no change will occur (Marstrand and Rush, 1978).

Without dogmatically asserting that significant man-induced climatic change will occur, it is important to explore some of the implications were it to happen. With reference to atmospheric carbon dioxide, Hare (1980, p. 392) comments:

If the build-up continues, and a doubling of concentration is achieved (conceivably by 2030 AD, but probably after 2050 AD), major climatic changes will ensue ... simulations indicate significant increases of rainfall. Such changes would be highly uneven, some regions becoming drier and some wetter. The implied climatic changes – to be achieved within a century – are larger than any observed in the past 10,000 years of terrestrial history.

The second reason for concern about the possibility of climatic change is the unusual number of extreme events recorded since 1960. The European Communities Commission (1978) noted thirty in the period up to 1976, ranging from the Sahel drought of 1968–73 to the first twentieth-century occurrence of sea ice around Iceland in 1975. With the fickleness of fashion, fears have alternated between the advance of the deserts and the onset of a new ice age. The generally accepted view is that the succession of unusually hot or cold, wet or dry periods experienced worldwide is within the normal range of climatic variation and does not presage a 'permanent' change, other than might occur *in the future* on account of human interference.

Third and last is the accumulating evidence of environmental degradation in the arid regions of *all* the world's continents. The extent of this problem is indicated in Figure 19. The symptoms are impoverishment of the vegetation cover, soil erosion and, in some areas, advance of sand dunes. A major debate now focuses on the question: is this impoverishment – widely known as desertification – due to man's misuse of the environment, or is it due to exogenous environmental changes? The preponderant view at present is that overgrazing, inept cultivation practices and the like are the probable cause, rather than any permanent climatic deterioration (Glantz, 1977a). On the other hand, this possibility cannot be dismissed.

At the present time, we do not know enough about the global interrelationships of atmospheric circulation and the regimes of the oceans and ice caps to make confident predictions about the magnitude and nature of possible climatic changes within the next century or so. However, in the light of the build-up of atmospheric carbon dioxide, it is worth considering the implications of a general rise in temperatures of the order 1°C to 2°C, which appears to be within the realms of possibility and would constitute a climatic alteration of a magnitude contemplated by Hare (1980). Even a less substantial change, of the magnitude actually experienced within the last three hundred years in Western Europe, would nevertheless be quite appreciable:

Lamb has suggested that changes of average summer temperature in central England between the warmest and coolest decades of the past three centuries represents shifts between conditions typical for northern France

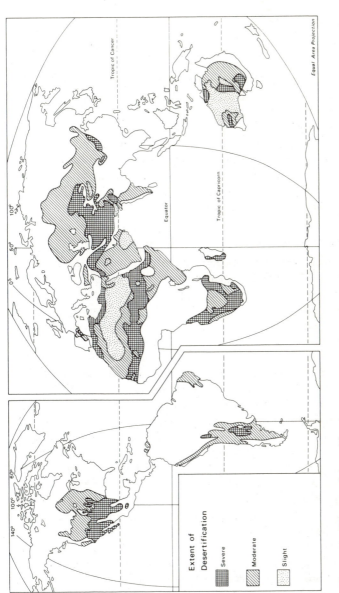

Figure 19 *Extent of desertification*
Source: Hare (1980).

and lowland Scotland; and changes of decade average winter temperature range from conditions typical for eastern Ireland to those typical for western Holland. (Parry, 1978, pp. 19–20)

It is widely believed that were there to be a general rise of between 1°C and 2°C in atmospheric temperature, the increase would be substantially greater in high latitudes and less in low latitudes (Cabinet Office, 1980). There would also be significant shifts in precipitation patterns. As yet, it is impossible to make confident predictions regarding the nature of these changes, though manifestly they are likely to be of much greater significance for the marginal regions of the world than for regions with a more generous climate. These marginal regions include some of the world's poorest countries, which would be affected (adversely or favourably) by events taking place outside their borders.

Effects of climatic change: the world's marginal regions

The logical point of departure for analysing the economic significance of climatic change would appear to be the known relationship between seasonal and annual weather variations and economic phenomena of various kinds. Unfortunately there are two fundamental problems with this approach. Short-term fluctuations in either or both temperature and precipitation do not permit economic and social adjustments to be made that would occur were a perceptible permanent change to happen. An unusually cold winter raises fuel bills. However, in countries accustomed to very cold winters, the design and construction of premises is such that comfort can be maintained without the consumption of enormous quantities of fuel, whereas in warmer climes less insulation is used. Similarly, agricultural practices can adjust to expected conditions if a pattern of recurrence has been established; by contrast, a short run of unexpected seasonal conditions can cause a calamity. The second problem is that only for some sectors can a reasonably accurate correlation between weather conditions and economic performance be established. While the connection between winter temperatures and fuel consumption is fairly precisely known for advanced economies, it is much harder to determine the implications of temperature and precipitation variation of agricultural output and other forms of activity (Maunder, 1970; Takahashi and Yoshino, 1978). Therefore, we must be circumspect in our approach to this problem.

A basic distinction must be made between modern industrial economies on the one hand, and agriculturally based economies on the other – especially those that are very poor and coping with conditions that are marginal for agricultural pursuits. Initially, we will consider the former group of countries. For these nations, climatic change of the scale we are envisaging would have trivial economic repercussions. The Cabinet Office (1980) has recently reported on the possible effect of changes in temperature and precipitation on the economy of the United Kingdom. A variation of about 10 per cent in annual or seasonal precipitation would have little effect on agriculture or other sectors, but a change of between 1°C and 2°C in the annual average temperature would have an appreciable, though quite small, impact on the economy. Compared with a maximum divergence of 0.4°C from the mean annual temperature over the period 1941–70, a 1°C change would be quite large. A 1°C decrease in annual temperature would lead to higher annual primary fuel consumption of about £200 million at 1977 prices, which, in terms of final users' expenditure, might make a difference of about £300 million. If winters become colder, to match the conditions of 1978–9, then additional snow clearance and gritting costs would be about £30 million, plus an extra £50 million for road repairs. In addition, the construction industry would incur higher costs; with a total annual expenditure of approximately £16,000 million, a 1 per cent increase in costs would be £160 million. These figures must be viewed in the context of total GDP for 1977 amounting to £110,000 million. The figure for increased fuel consumption (£200 million) is equivalent to 0.002 per cent of GDP, which is very much less than the 0.15 per cent that can be derived from Manley's (1957) data for the difference between a very mild winter and spring, and a very severe season. It seems reasonable to suggest that if, instead of a 1°C reduction in temperature, there were an equivalent rise, the annual savings would be of the same magnitude. In this case, however, it is likely that the polar ice caps would be reduced somewhat and additional expenditure on sea defences would be required to cope with higher sea levels. The Cabinet Office estimates that it would cost £1000 million to raise sea defences 0.75 metres but points out that this expenditure could be spread over several decades.

With respect to agriculture, it is useful to turn to Japan, for which country some informative studies have recently been carried out. Takahashi and Nemoto (1978) estimate that for Japan as a whole a

1°C difference in the annual average temperature results in a 20–30 per cent variation in total rice output. This variation is spread differentially, with a much larger crop variation in the north of the country than in the south. Furthermore, temperatures are less reliable in the north of the country than in the south, as is well demonstrated by Uchijima (1978). Taking 10°C as the threshold, he calculated the relationship between accumulated degree days and rice yields. He was able to estimate the frequency of deviations of a given relative magnitude in the sum of degree days for several regions. For a drop in temperature such as could be expected once in five, ten, twenty, thirty and forty years, he estimated the decline in yields. For a thirty-year recurrence period, rice production in Hokkaido would be only 57 per cent of the norm, whereas in southerly Kanto-Tozan the yield would be 97 per cent. Clearly, rice production in northerly Japan is much more vulnerable to reduction in temperatures than is the case in more southerly latitudes.

Japan is a relatively favoured country, in the sense that its climate is fairly reliable. India, by contrast, is highly dependent upon the summer monsoon, which appears to have become less dependable since 1964. Taking the average of the period 1947–75, Saha and Mooley (1978) have calculated the fraction of India's area over which the summer monsoon rainfall is less than 80 per cent of the norm. The results are shown in Figure 20. On the evidence of a limited statistical test, the impact of precipitation variation on crop yields seemed less than one might have expected. But, as the authors point out, total summer rainfall is only one variable and a more sophisticated analysis than they were able to undertake seems to be called for.

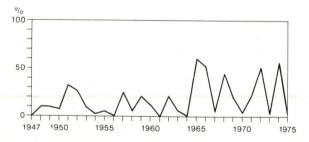

Figure 20   *Percentage area of India over which the summer monsoon rain was less than 80 per cent of the average for the period 1947–75* Source: Saha and Mooley (1978).

For countries such as Britain and Japan, farmers would be able to adjust to climatic change in a number of different ways. Substitution between products could occur. For example, were rice growing in northern Japan to become uneconomic, wheat cultivation would probably be a viable alternative. Similarly, were grain cultivation in the less-favoured arable areas of Britain to be threatened by lower temperatures and higher precipitation, potatoes or grass would be options to consider. An alternative strategy would be to adopt crop and animal varieties specially bred for the new climatic conditions. Adjustments in farming practice would be relatively straightforward in all the advanced industrial nations and also in countries such as Australia and New Zealand, being nations with commercial farming backed by a good infrastructure of research and breeding stations. Even so, there would be very serious problems in the dryer crop and livestock regions were precipitation to decline to any appreciable extent, since the options for substitution and selective breeding are limited. The position would be very much more difficult in poorer nations, highly dependent on agriculture, lacking the necessary infrastructure of research, and with a conservative, illiterate peasantry.

Two main categories of marginal region can be identified – the hot arid lands of the tropics and continental interiors, and the cold regions of high latitudes. Water supply and temperature are, respectively, the critical limiting factors. Notwithstanding the large amount of climatic information that has accumulated during the last century, the division of the world into climatic regions remains at least as much an art as a science. This is particularly true when attempts are made to describe the multitude of local/regional climates in terms of a relatively small number of categories, suitable for reproduction in black and white in a book such as the present one (see Figure 21). However, if we compare Trewartha (1954 and 1961) with Strahler (1969), Landsberg *et al.* (1965) and UNESCO (1979), we note that the classifications offered àre lineal descendants of Köppen's work, and that there is broad correspondence between the world-wide patterns identified. As with Thornthwaite's (1948) system, the classifications are based on conditions relevant for plant growth, and hence for agriculture, pastoralism and forestry.

The general correspondence between the regions of the world which experience dry climates (Figure 21) and the areas where desertification is evident (Figure 19, p. 179) is indeed striking. In some cases, the existence of rivers makes possible cultivation that

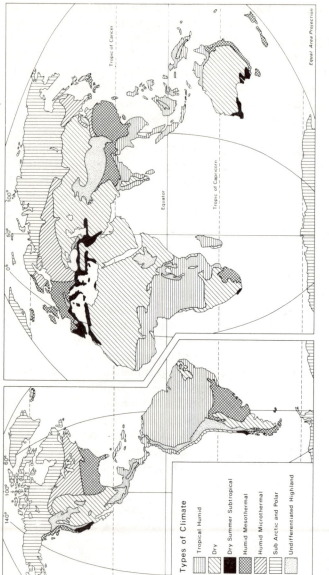

Figure 21   *Climatic regions of the world*
Source: Trewartha (1961).

otherwise would be impracticable; the Nile, Tigris, Euphrates and Indus (plus tributaries) are the four most important examples. Analogous, though less significant, examples occur world-wide, as for example along the arid coastal belt of Chile and Peru, and in Russia south of the Aral Sea. Table 32 has been compiled to summarize the global situation with respect to aridity. A UNESCO map of the world distribution of arid climates has been used to assign countries to two categories, wholly arid and having substantial dry areas. This classification is necessarily rough and ready, but it serves to show that about 290 million people live in countries which are virtually entirely arid, about 7 per cent of the world's total. Some 2460 million, or 60 per cent of all mankind, live in countries which contain substantial areas of aridity. In addition, a small number of countries can be classed as wholly or substantially cold, but the only really large population is in the USSR. Viewed in global terms, the sensitive regions are the dry ones, where a change of either precipitation or temperature, or both, could have dramatic effects.

According to investigations at the University of East Anglia and elsewhere (*New Scientist*, 9 April 1981), if there were a general warming of the atmosphere, it is likely that the chief wheat and maize producing regions of the USA and USSR would be adversely affected – by lower precipitation as well as higher temperatures. At the same time, the rice-growing areas of Asia would be likely to benefit. While America could accommodate a reduction in grain output, the repercussions on international trade could be serious. Most of the grain which enters international commerce comes from North America and the greatest losers would be the USSR and countries of the Third World which at present cannot feed their population and depend substantially on imports.

It would be premature to jump to conclusions at this stage. However, the evidence is now compelling that environmental, and especially climatic, changes have been occurring throughout the historical period and to a degree sufficient to have an impact on the wealth of nations in at least some parts of the world – and especially those which are climatically marginal. Since the greater part of Western Europe is decidedly not marginal, a Eurocentric view of the situation is wholly inappropriate in the present context. Inhabitants of the Sahel will note that some 4000–6000 years ago most of what is now the Sahara desert was open grassland carrying game. Yet, the third major drought of the present century (1968–73) saw the death of 100,000 people, or 2 per cent of the susceptible population, and a

Table 32   *The arid nations of the world, with populations c.1978 (millions)*

Wholly arid areas		Substantial arid areas	
Country	*Population*	*Country*	*Population*
Afghanistan	15.1	Argentina	26.4
Algeria	18.5	Australia	14.2
Bahrain	0.3	Chile	10.9
Botswana	0.7	China	975.2
Chad	4.3	Ethiopia	29.7
Djibouti	0.1	Gambia	0.6
Egypt	41.0	Guinea–Bissau	0.8
Iran	35.2	India	638.4
Iraq	12.3	Kenya	14.9
Israel	3.7	Lesotho	1.3
Jordan	3.0	Madagascar	8.3
Kuwait	1.2	Mexico	66.9
Lebanon	3.0	Mongolia	1.6
Libyan Arab Republic	2.7	Morocco	18.9
Mali	6.3	Mozambique	11.8
Mauritania	1.5	Peru	16.8
Namibia	0.9	South Africa	27.7
Niger	5.0	Spain	37.1
Oman	0.8	Tanzania	16.6
Pakistan	76.8	Tunisia	6.1
Qatar	0.2	Turkey	43.2
Saudi Arabia	7.9	Uganda	12.8
Senegal	5.4	USSR	263.4
Somali Republic	3.4	USA	218.1
Sudan	17.4		
Swaziland	0.5	*Total*	2461.1
Syrian Arab Republic	8.1		
United Arab Emirates	0.7		
Upper Volta	6.6		
Western Sahara	0.1		
Yemen (North)	5.6		
Yemen (South)	1.9		
Total	290.8		

Note: Table compiled by Mr D. A. Stewart, Department of Geography, University of Cambridge.

Sources: UNESCO (1979); Fullard (1972), pp. 11–16.

catastrophic 40 per cent of the cattle, prime symbol and source of wealth (Glantz, 1977b). Mortality among the human population would have been higher but for international relief and migration of the stricken peoples to neighbouring better-favoured areas. The future prosperity or poverty of these people is closely and directly linked to the amount of rain; for them, it is literally a matter of life or death whether any change that does occur in their climatic environment is favourable or adverse. Many millions elsewhere in the world share this immediate concern with possible global climatic change.

Conclusion

One of the great problems with the subject surveyed in this chapter is the recency of a reasonably reliable chronology of historical climatic change even for Europe, and the longevity of older and superseded chronologies. Parry (1978) notes that Slicher van Bath (1963) used an inaccurate climatic compilation dating from 1937, which appears to be corroborated by the work of Brooks. Thus, some of the important and influential attempts to relate climatic change to historical development have, inadvertently, used misleading evidence. Possibly much more important has been the failure of historians to recognize the significance of temperature and precipitation thresholds, and the related failure to distinguish marginal regions, where small changes of climate may be very significant, from non-marginal areas where even quite large changes may have but a small impact. Looking at the world as a whole, this last distinction appears to be crucial.

Underlying this problem is 'the hazardous nature of an essay in cross-disciplinary studies' to which Anderson (1978, p. 310) referred. The dangers are manifest in the stance adopted by Wallerstein (1974, pp. 34–5) in his consideration of the crisis of feudalism in the fourteenth and fifteenth centuries in Europe. Noting that climatic deterioration might provide an explanation he says:

... this hypothesis must be taken seriously. Certainly some of the fourteenth century abandonments of cultivation (cereals in Iceland, the Scandinavian colonies in Greenland, the lowest forest limit in Sudetenland, the end of viticulture in England and its regression in Germany) are all plausibly explained by climatic change. But there are alternative plausible explanations. Most importantly, Duby reminds us that 'agrarian recession, like the demographic collapse, started before the beginning of the fourteenth century', hence before the presumed climatic changes. Instead, Duby would see climatic factors and then epidemiology as being cumulative woes which, in the fourteenth century, 'dealt a crushing blow to the already fragile demographic structure'. . . .

Obviously, to the extent that there was climatic change, it would affect the operation of a social system. Yet equally obviously, it would affect different systems differently. Though opinions differ, it is probable that such glaciation as did occur was spread over the whole Northern Hemisphere, yet social developments in Asia and North America were clearly divergent from those in Europe. It would be useful therefore to return to the chronic factor of resource strain involved in the feudal system of social organisation, or overconsumption by a minority given the overall low level of productivity.

In this passage, Wallerstein makes the same kinds of mistake made by Huntington, though in the reverse direction, and supporting the opposite conclusion (see p. 169). That is, he assumes the simultaneity of climatic change across the globe and, on the basis of limited evidence, dismisses the climatic factor whereas Huntington argued for its importance.

As the twentieth century draws to a close, a whole new field of contemporary and historical inquiry has been opened up. As yet, it is impossible to establish securely the chains of causation – the origin of climatic change and its consequences for various peoples. However, it does seem clear that it is no longer proper to ignore exogenous environmental change as a possible major influence on the long-term prosperity of nations.

7 Perspective

There is a history in all men's lives,
Figuring the nature of the times deceas'd;
The which observ'd a man may prophesy,
With a near aim of the main chance of things
As yet not come to life, which in their seeds
And weak beginnings lie intreasured.

(William Shakespeare, *King Henry IV, Part II*, Harrap, 1927)

An extended essay such as the present volume does not lend itself to clean and neat conclusions, the more so because of the complexity and wide-ranging nature of the subject. Just as it is vain to seek a *primum mobile* as the basic cause of wealth and progress, so is it impractical to expect to find a single answer to our central question: why is it that some nations are richer or poorer than others?

The reader will have noted that I take an optimistic view of the world's growth process. I do not visualize any necessary reason why over-all growth will cease, nor any necessary reason why the poor nations must remain poor for ever. On the other hand, there is, equally, no necessity for growth to spread to all peoples, no certainty that improved standards of living will in fact be achieved. However, the long historical evidence, and recent post-war experience, leaves little doubt that a substantial improvement has been apparent for a large, and growing, proportion of humanity. This same historical evidence suggests that there is a great deal of continuity, over decades and even centuries, and that therefore it is unrealistic to expect a sudden transformation from poverty to wealth, except for a lucky few benefiting from some bonanza such as oil provides. For the great majority of men, prosperity depends on the ability of the society in which they live to respond to the opportunities that are available. While it is clearly true that the international economy has had differential effects on the nations of the world, some beneficial and some disadvantageous, it is clear that the 'system' (whether described as capitalist or otherwise) cannot be blamed as a general cause of poverty. This is not to deny that some countries, especially the smaller members of the Third World, are influenced by external events to a much greater extent than are members of the world's core. But this is only a matter of degree, since all nations are to some extent interdependent with others and, in some measure, must adapt to the rest of the world as they find it. Both the USA and USSR have discovered that there are serious constraints to the imposition of their will on other nations. Following Russia's invasion of Afghanistan in 1980, and the war between Iran and Iraq, America attempted to cajole the Gulf States into an alliance to ensure the unhindered transit of oil, marking yet another chapter in the long history of attempts to maintain a dominant position in the region. Similarly, the explosion of unrest in Poland in 1980 provided Russia with a set of very delicate problems, in which it proved impossible immediately to impose her will and control the unfolding of events. Both the superpowers, and China, have found that their attempts to buy friends through the provision of aid and armaments is a dangerous, two-edged game, in which the nominally client states may throw out one and invite in another. Collectively, the developing countries exert pressure on the richer nations with respect to such issues as trade and price arrangements, and the provision of credit – pressure which the core nations cannot afford to ignore, even if they also are unwilling to accede in full.

We have used the core-periphery model as a useful framework within which to consider worldwide patterns of development. As argued on p. 60, this binary classification is not immutable; the group of nations comprising the core has expanded over time. The growth processes which are evident in the core nations owe a great deal to the continuing progress of science and technology, and the associated development of new 'propulsive' industries, whether these be cotton textiles in the early industrial revolution, electricity and chemical industries at the end of the nineteenth century, vehicles during the first half of the present century or, prospectively, the constellation of industries based on microchips, computers, etc. For these countries, the future course of events cannot be predicted, other than at a very general level. There is now a sufficiently large number of core nations, competing in rather similar products, that technological advance in one must be matched in the others, unless they are content to see their living standards fall in relation to the other advanced countries. Symptomatic of this process is the commanding lead established by Japan in the use of industrial robots. Similarly, it is to the Japanese steel industry that the British Steel Corporation has turned for help in modernizing the British industry.

A large majority of the world's population still lives outside the core nations, in what we have called the periphery. There is a wide divergence of view regarding the impact of the core upon the periphery. At the very least, the relationship between core and periphery has been complex. The proposition that the core has exploited the periphery, and that the penetration of the international economy into peripheral nations has caused their present state of underdevelopment, cannot be sustained as a general process on the evidence available. Undoubtedly many effects have been harmful, but equally there have been important impulses to development which have had tangible beneficial effects. Of these, the first was associated with the nineteenth-century colonization of temperate lands in the northern and southern hemisphere. This paved the way for the emergence of a small group of countries as prosperous members of the international community. Somewhat later, the growth in demand for tropical foodstuffs and materials provided an important impetus for a much larger group of countries, but this impetus was small relative to the populations concerned and served primarily to lay the foundations for the future, rather than to generate tangible progress for the masses during the earlier part of the present century. Since the last world war, however, that groundwork has proved its value and the progress that has been achieved since then would have been much harder of attainment in its absence.

Since the second world war, two other groups of nations have come forth from the international wings. Industry-led development has been notably successful in countries such as South Korea and Taiwan, and to a lesser extent in Mexico and Brazil, and elsewhere. The long-term prospects for these nations must be regarded as good, provided only that the international community will keep export opportunities open and that the countries themselves can maintain and improve their technological capacity to adjust to changing international circumstances. The second group is the nations rich in non-renewable resources, other than those included in the groups already mentioned. The fundamental problem for these countries is the relatively short-lived nature of their opportunity and the need to convert the temporary profits into long-term assets. For a country such as Nigeria, with excellent agricultural potential, the wise use of oil revenues could pave the way for continuing prosperity; export-led industrialization need not be the route that must be followed. Semi-desert and desert states, on the other hand, will find that they have immense difficulties. Agriculture cannot be the mainstay of their economies and they must find export activities, whether in manufactures or services. The choice must depend, in part at least, upon location: for example, ship repair and servicing, and international air communications, are both highly relevant for the Persian Gulf nations, but could not be of much utility to the land-locked states of the Sahel. Herein lies a cruel irony, in that to make this leap requires the people to engage in a breakneck process of economic and social transformation, that would test the fabric of any society.

The last group of countries that we have identified comprises those with very large populations and a high degree of dependence upon agriculture. By virtue of their very size, and the dispersed nature of development implied by an agricultural economy, they must depend very largely upon their own efforts and resources. Perhaps the single most important need that they have is help in devising technology appropriate to their conditions of physical and social environment. In this respect, the core nations have potentially an important role to play. However effective this and other help may be, and however well these large countries may organize their affairs, progress is almost certain to be slow for many decades. There cannot be a quick improvement, notwithstanding that one wishes there could be.

If, by the middle of the next century, China, India, and the other very populous but presently poor nations have achieved steady and sustainable growth, and if the export-led industrialization of some other smaller states has been maintained, two major question marks are likely to remain. How successful will those countries that have a short-lived opportunity provided by non-renewable resources be in breaking out of poverty? And what will happen to the residue of countries, lacking the advantages of such resources and currently at a very low level of development? Will they be dependent on the charity of others, or will there be yet another impulse to development of which they can take advantage, but of which we are, as yet, unaware? From the vantage of the 1980s, there is no way in which we can offer an answer to these questions.

The reader will have noticed that much more emphasis has been accorded to natural resources and to cultural factors than is customary at the present time. Part of the reason arises from the attention which has been given to long-term as against short-term processes of development. Part also arises from our review of previous thought and the awareness engendered thereby of the over-hasty abandonment of earlier beliefs. Perhaps more important than either, but underlying both, is the geographer's awareness of the differences that exist from place to place, which have persisted for generations and millennia, and which cannot be wished away. The optimism of the 1950s and 1960s that Western technology could be exported ready-made, and that industrialization would provide a quick route to prosperity, has now given way to a much more realistic assessment of the rate of change that is possible given the environmental and socio-economic constraints. The pre-eminence of industrialization as the route to greater wealth is no longer maintained as a universal basis for policy. In many countries, and especially the larger, poor and populous ones, much more attention is being given to agriculture. There is a desperate need to achieve or maintain self-sufficiency in foodstuffs and thereby economize on foreign exchange. In addition, the size of the domestic market for manufactures and services of all kinds depends in large measure on the level of agricultural incomes and hence productivity on the farms.

The realization that for many, though not all, of the countries in the Third World the key to prosperity lies in agriculture, carries an important implication. The circumstances of Europe in the eighteenth century provide some important parallels. In particular, classical economic thought has a degree of relevance for much of the Third World that it does not have for the core nations of the world, especially the interest in land resources.

Culture as a variable affecting the development process is impossible to quantify. As with land resources, the utility of particular characteristics may change over time. The individualism which characterized the emergence of Europe allowed a great deal of energy to be creatively employed. For all the ifs and buts of history, it seems unlikely that the industrial revolution and the modern technological era could have occurred in the absence of individual freedom to speculate, to investigate and to construct. With the evolution of modern industrial economies, it is not self-evident that these traits of individuality are the most suitable for maintaining and advancing modern civilization. It may be that societies with a tradition for cooperative endeavour are better adapted for the present phase of history. If this is so, then there are some important implications for domestic policies in many of today's more advanced countries.

We are straying into the realm of speculation. However, the speculation with which we will conclude is as follows. The 1950s and 1960s witnessed a prodigious folly, that Man could conquer Nature and bend her to his will. The 1970s saw the dawning awareness that at the global scale Nature might wreak a terrible revenge, unless Man adapted to the constraints imposed by the natural environment. The same lesson is now being learned at the sub-global scale, at the level of nation states, with the additional complication that social and institutional realities must also be taken into account. We need to know far more about these realities than we do at present, and how to adapt technology to the circumstances we find. Because technology and institutions change, and because the world has a geography – which itself is changing – we do indeed have work for all time.

Bibliography

ABEL, W. (1980), *Agricultural Fluctuations in Europe: From the Thirteenth to the Twentieth Centuries*, Methuen (first published 1935)

ADELMAN, M. A. (1964), 'The world oil outlook', in M. Clawson (ed.), *Natural Resources and International Development*, Johns Hopkins University Press, pp. 27–125

AL-SAYARI, S. S. and ZÖTL, J. G. (eds.) (1978), *Quaternary Period in Saudi Arabia*, Springer-Verlag

AMIN, S. (1973), *Neo-Colonialism in West Africa*, Penguin (first published in French 1971)

ANDERSON, J. L. (1978), 'Climate and the historians', in A. B. Pittock, *et al.* (eds.), *Climatic Change and Variability: A Southern Perspective*, Cambridge University Press, pp. 310–16

ARMSTRONG, T., *et al.* (1978), *The Circumpolar North*, Methuen

ARNDT, H. W. (1978), *The Rise and Fall of Economic Growth: A Study in Contemporary Thought*, Longman

ASHWORTH, W. (1960), *An Economic History of England 1870–1939*, Methuen

ASHWORTH, W. (1975), *A Short History of the International Economy since 1850*, 3rd edn, Longman

AUTY, R. M. (1979), 'Worlds within the Third World', *Area*, vol. 11, pp. 232–5

BAGCHI, A. K. (1972), *Private Investment in India 1900–1939*, Cambridge University Press

BAIROCH, P. (1975), *The Economic Development of the Third World since 1900*, Methuen

BALASSA, B., *et al.* (1971), *The Structure of Protection in Developing Countries*, Johns Hopkins University Press

Bank of New South Wales Review, (1980), 'Capital requirements in the 1980s', no. 33, pp. 3–12

BAUER, P. T. and YAMEY, B. S. (1957), *The Economics of Under-Developed Countries*, Cambridge University Press

BECKER, J. F. (1977), *Marxian Political Economy: An Outline*, Cambridge University Press

BLAINEY, G. (1970), 'A theory of mineral discovery: Australia in the nineteenth century', *Economic History Review*, vol. 23, pp. 298–313

BOSERUP, E. (1965), *The Conditions of Agricultural Growth: The Economics of Agrarian Change under Population Pressure*, Allen and Unwin

BOSSON, R. and BENSION, V. (1977), *The Mining Industry and the Developing Countries*, Oxford University Press

BRADBURY, ·J. H. (1979), 'Towards an alternative theory of resource-based town development in Canada', *Economic Geography*, vol. 55, pp. 147–66

Brandt Report (1980); *North–South: a programme for survival*, report of Independent Commission on International Issues under the Chairmanship of Willy Brandt, Pan Books

BRAUDEL, F. (1949), *La Mediterranée et le Monde mediterranéen à l'époque de Philippe II*, Armand Colin (English edn published by Collins 1972)

BRAUDEL, F. (1972), 'History and the social sciences', in P. Burke (ed.), *Economy and Society in Early Modern Europe*, Routledge and Kegan Paul, pp. 11–42 (first published in French 1958)

BREWER, A. (1980), *Marxist Theories of Imperialism: A Critical Survey*, Routledge and Kegan Paul

BRICE, W. C. (ed.) (1978), *The Environmental History of the Near and Middle East since the Last Ice Age*, Academic Press

BROOKE, M. Z. (1970), *Le Play: Engineer and Social Scientist*, Longman

BROOKS, C. E. P. (1925), *The Evolution of Climate*, Ernest Benn

BROOKS, C. E. P. (1949), *Climate through the Ages: A Study of the Climatic Factors and their Variations*, Ernest Benn (first published 1926)

BROWN, L. A. and MOORE, E. G. (1969), 'Diffusion research in geography: a perspective', in C. Board, *et al.* (eds.), *Progress in Geography*, vol. 1, Arnold, pp. 119–57

BRÜCKNER, E. (1890), 'Die Klimaschwankungen seit 1700', *Geographische Abhandlungen*, vol. 4

BRUTON, H. J. (1960), 'Contemporary theorizing on economic growth', in B. Hoselitz, *et al.*, pp. 239–98

BRYAN, P. W. (1933), *Man's Adaptation of Nature: Studies of the Cultural Landscape*, University of London Press

BRYSON, R. A. and MURRAY, T. J. (1977), *Climates of Hunger: Mankind and the World's Changing Weather*, University of Wisconsin Press

BUTTRICK, J. (1960), 'Toward a theory of economic growth: the neoclassical contribution', in B. F. Hoselitz, *et al.*, pp. 155–92

BUTZER, K. W. (1970), 'Physical conditions in Eastern Europe, Western Asia and Egypt before the period of agricultural and urban settlement', in I. E. S. Edwards *et al.* (eds.), *The Cambridge Ancient History*, 3rd edn, vol. 1, Cambridge University Press, pp. 35–69

Cabinet Office (1980), *Climatic Change: Its potential effects on the United Kingdom and the Implications for Research*, HMSO

CAIRNCROSS, A. K. (1962), *Factors in Economic Development*, Allen and Unwin

CALDWELL, M. (1977), *The Wealth of Some Nations*, Zed Press

CAMERON, E. N. (ed.) (1973), *The Mineral Position of the United States, 1975–2000*, University of Wisconsin Press

CARPENTER, R. (1966), *Discontinuity in Greek Civilization*, Cambridge University Press

CAVES, R. E. and HOLTON, R. H. (1959), *The Canadian Economy: Prospect and Retrospect*, Harvard University Press

CHARLESWORTH, J. K. (1957), *The Quaternary Era with Special Reference to its Glaciation*, Arnold

CHENERY, H (1979), *Structural Change and Development Policy*, Oxford University Press

CHENERY, H. and SYRQUIN, M. (1975), *Patterns of Development, 1950–1970*, Oxford University Press

CHENERY, H. and TAYLOR, L. (1968), 'Development patterns: among countries and over time', *Review of Economics and Statistics*, vol. 50, pp. 391–416

CHISHOLM, M. (1966), *Geography and Economics*, Bell

CHISHOLM, M. (1977), 'Regional growth theory, location theory, non-renewable natural resources and the mobile factors of production', in B. Ohlin, *et al.* (eds.), *The International Allocation of Economic Activity: Proceedings of a Nobel Symposium*, Macmillan, pp. 103–14

CHISHOLM, M. (1979), *Rural Settlement and Land Use: an Essay in Location*, 3rd edn, Hutchinson

CHISHOLM, M. (1980), 'The wealth of nations', *Transactions*, Institute of British Geographers, New Series, vol. 5, pp. 255–76

CLAPHAM, J. H. (1922), 'Of empty economic boxes', *Economic Journal*, vol. 32, pp. 305–14

CLARK, C. (1940), *The Conditions of Economic Progress*, Macmillan

CLARK, C. (1967), *Population Growth and Land Use*, Macmillan

CLIFF, A. D., *et al.* (1981), *Spatial Diffusion: A Historical Geography of Epidemics in an Island Community*, Cambridge University Press

COTTRELL, P. L. (1980), *Industrial Finance 1830–1914: The Finance and Organisaton of English Manufacturing Industry*, Methuen

CROWSON, P. (1977), *British Foreign Policy to 1985: Non-Fuel Minerals and Foreign Policy*, Royal Institute of International Affairs

CROWSON, P. (1979), 'The geography and political economy of metal supplies', *Resources Policy*, vol. 5, pp. 158–69

DEANE, P. (1978), *The Evolution of Economic Ideas*, Cambridge University Press

DEANE, P. and COLE, W. A. (1967), *British Economic Growth 1688–1959: Trends and Structure*, Cambridge University Press

DENISON, E. F. (1962), *The Sources of Economic Growth in the United States and the Alternatives Before Us*, Committee for Economic Development

DENISON, E. F. (1967), *Why Growth Rates Differ: Postwar Experience in Nine Western Countries*, Brookings Institution

Department of Mines and Resources (1947), *Geology and Economic Minerals of Canada*, King's Printer and Controller of Stationery

EAGLY, R. V. (1974), *The Structure of Classical Economic Theory*, Oxford University Press

EARNEY, F. C. F. (1980), *Petroleum and Hard Minerals from the Sea*, Arnold

EL MALLAKH, R. (1979), *Qatar: Development of an Oil Economy*, Croom Helm

European Communities Commission (1978), 'Taming the climate: EEC climatic research programme proposed', *Background Report*, 20 October 1978, ECC

EYRE, S. R. (1978), *The Real Wealth of Nations*, Arnold

FAIRGRIEVE, J. (1927), *Geography and World Power*, University of London Press (first published 1915)

FIELDHOUSE, D. K. (1973), *Economics and Empire 1830–1914*, Weidenfeld and Nicolson

FISHLOW, A., *et al.* (1978), *Rich and Poor Nations in the World Economy*, McGraw-Hill

FRANK, A. G. (1964), 'On the mechanisms of imperialism: the case of Brazil', *Monthly Review*, vol. 16, pp. 284–97

FRANK, A. G. (1966), 'The development of underdevelopment' *Monthly Review*, vol. 18, pp. 17–31

FRANK, A. G. (1967), *Capitalism and Underdevelopment in Latin America: Historical Studies of Chile and Brazil*, Monthly Review Press

FREEMAN, C. and JAHODA, M. (eds.) (1978), *World Futures: The Great Debate*, Robertson

FRITTS, H. C. (1976), *Tree Rings and Climate*, Academic Press

FULLARD, N. (1972), *The Geographical Digest 1972*, Philip

FURNIVALL, J. S. (1948), *Colonial Policy and Practice: A Comparative Study of Burma and Netherlands India*, Cambridge University Press

FURTADO, C. (1964), *Development and Underdevelopment*, University of California Press

GALTON, F. (1883), *Inquiries into Human Faculty and its Development*, Cassell

General Agreement on Tariffs and Trade (1958), *Trends in International Trade: Report by a Panel of Experts*, GATT

General Agreement on Tariffs and Trade (1978), *Networks of World Trade by Areas and Commodity Classes, 1955–1976*, GATT

GEORGE, H. B. (1930), *The Relations of Geography and History*, Clarendon Press (first edn 1901)

GEORGESCU-ROEGAN, N. (1971), *The Entropy Law and the Economic Process*, Harvard University Press

GINSBURG, N. (1957), 'Natural resources and economic development', *Annals*, Association of American Geographers, vol. 47, pp. 197–212

GLACKEN, C. J. (1967), *Traces on the Rhodian Shore: Nature and Culture in Western Thought from Ancient Times to the End of the Eighteenth Century*, University of California Press

GLAMANN, K. (1971), *European Trade 1500–1750*, Fontana Economic History of Europe

GLAMANN, K. (1977), 'The changing patterns of trade', in E. E. Rich and C. H. Wilson (eds.), *The Cambridge Economic History of Europe*, vol. 5, *The Economic Organization of Early Modern Europe*, Cambridge University Press, pp. 185–289

GLANTZ, M. H. (ed.) (1977a), *Desertification: Environmental Degradation in and Around Arid Lands*, Westview Press

GLANTZ, M. H. (1977b), 'The UN and desertification: dealing with a global problem', in M. H. Glantz (ed.), *Desertification: Environmental Degradation in and Around Arid Lands*, Westview Press, pp. 1–15

GOUDIE, A. (1977), *Environmental Change*, Clarendon Press

GOULD, J. D. (1972), *Economic Growth in History: Survey and Analysis*, Methuen

GOUROU, P. (1958), *The Tropical World*, Longman (first published in French 1947)

GOVETT, M. H. (1975), 'The geographic concentration of world mineral supplies', *Resources Policy*, vol. 1, pp. 357–70

GOVETT, M. H. (1976), 'Geographic concentration of world mineral supplies, production and consumption', in G. J. S. Govett and M. H. Govett (eds.), *World Mineral Supplies: Assessment and Perspective*, Elsevier, pp. 99–145

GRIGG, D. (1979), 'Ester Boserup's theory of agrarian change: a critical review', *Progress in Human Geography*, vol. 3, pp. 64–84

GROVE, J. M. (1972), 'The incidence of landslides, avalanches, and floods in western Norway during the little ice age', *Arctic and Alpine Research*, vol. 4, pp. 131–8

HÄGERSTRAND, T. (1967), *Innovation Diffusion as a Spatial Process*, University of Chicago Press (first published in Swedish in 1953)

HAGGETT, P. (1964), 'Regional and local components in the distribution of forested areas in south-east Brazil; a multivariate approach', *Geographical Journal*, vol. 130, pp. 365–78

HAGGETT, P. (1979), *Geography: A Modern Synthesis*, 3rd edn, Harper and Row

HAHN, F. H. and MATTHEWS R. C. O. (1965), 'The theory of economic growth: a survey', in American Economic Association and Royal Economic Society, *Surveys of Economic Theory*, vol. 2, *Growth and Development*, Macmillan, pp. 1–124

HALL, P. (ed.) (1966), *Von Thünen's Isolated State*, Pergamon

HARE, F. K. (1980), 'The planetary environment: fragile or sturdy?' *Geographical Journal*, vol. 146, pp. 379–95

HILFERDING, R. (1970), *Le Capital Financier*, Editions de Minuit (first published in German 1910)

HIRSCHMAN, A. O. (1958), *The Strategy of Economic Development*, Yale University Press

HOBSON, J. A. (1948), *Imperialism: A Study*, Allen and Unwin (first published by James Nisbet and Co. 1902)

HOLLAND, S. (1976), *Capital Versus the Regions*, Macmillan

HOPKINS, A. G. (1973), *An Economic History of West Africa*, Longman

HOSELITZ, B. F. (1960), 'Theories of the stages of economic growth', in B. F. Hoselitz, *et al.*, pp. 193–238

HOSELITZ, B. F., *et al.* (1960), *Theories of Economic Growth*, Free Press of Glencoe

HUFBAUER, G. C. (1966), *Synthetic Materials and the Theory of International Trade*, Duckworth

HUNTINGTON, E. (1907), *The Pulse of Asia: A Journey in Central Asia Illustrating the Geographic Basis of History*, Houghton Mifflin

HUNTINGTON, E. (1915), *Civilization and Climate*, Yale University Press

HUNTINGTON, E. (1927), *The Character of Races as Influenced by Physical Environment, Natural Selection and Historical Development*, Scribner's

HUNTINGTON, E. (1945), *Mainsprings of Civilization*, Wiley

HYNES, W. G. (1979), *The Economics of Empire: Britain, Africa and the New Imperialism 1870–95*, Longman

IMLAH, A. H. (1958), *Economic Elements in the* Pax Britannica: *Studies in British Foreign Trade in the Nineteenth Century*, Harvard University Press

INNIS, H. A. (1930), *The Fur Trade in Canada: An Introduction to Canadian Economic History*, Yale University Press

INNIS, H. A. (1936), *Settlement and the Mining Frontier*, vol. 9, pt 2 of W. A. Mackintosh and W. L. G. Joerg (eds.), *Canadian Frontiers of Settlement*, Macmillan

ION, D. C. (1975), *Availability of World Energy Resources*, Graham and Trotman

ISHIKAWA, S. (1979), 'Appropriate technologies: some aspects of Japanese experience', in E. A. G. Robinson (ed.), pp. 75–132

JEVONS, W. S. (1865), *The Coal Question: An Inquiry Concerning the Progress of the Nation, and the Probable Exhaustion of our Coal-mines*, Macmillan

JEVONS, W. S. (1909), *Investigations in Currency and Finance*, ed. H. S. Foxwell, Macmillan (first published 1884)

JONES, G. T. (1933), *Increasing Return*, Cambridge University Press

JØRGENSEN, J. J. (1979), 'Structural dependence and the move to the left: the political economy of the Obote regime in Uganda', in T. M. Shaw and K. A. Heard (eds.), *The Politics of Africa: Dependence and Development*, Longman, pp. 43–72

JUTIKKALA, E. (1955), 'The Finnish famine in 1696–97', *The Scandinavian Economic History Review*, vol. 3, pp. 48–63

KAHN, H. (1979), *World Economic Development: 1979 and Beyond*, Croom Helm

KALDOR, N. (1967), *Strategic Factors in Economic Development*, Cornell University Press

KAMARCK, A. M. (1976), *The Tropics and Economic Development: A Provocative Enquiry into the Poverty of Nations*, Johns Hopkins University Press

KEYNES, J. M. (1926), *The End of Laissez-Faire*, Hogarth Press; reprinted in Royal Economic Society (1972), *The Collected Writings of John Maynard Keynes*, vol. 9, Macmillan, pp. 272–94

KEYNES, J. M. (1936), *The General Theory of Employment, Interest and Money*, Macmillan

KINDLEBERGER, C. P. (1956), *The Terms of Trade: A European Case Study*, MIT Press/Wiley

KINDLEBERGER, C. P. (1958), *Economic Development*, McGraw-Hill

KINDLEBERGER, C. P. (1962), *Foreign Trade and the National Economy*, Yale University Press

KINDLEBERGER, C. P. (1964), 'Terms of trade for primary products', in M. Clawson (ed.), *Natural Resources and International Development*, Johns Hopkins University Press, pp. 339–65

KONDRATIEFF, N. D. (1935), 'The long waves in economic life', *Review of Economic Statistics*, vol. 17, pp. 105–15

KRAVIS, I. B., et al. (1978), *International Comparisons of Real Product and Purchasing Power*, Johns Hopkins University Press

KUZNETS, S. (1966), *Modern Economic Growth: Rate, Structure and Spread*, Yale University Press

KUZNETS, S. (1971), *Economic Growth of Nations: Total Output and Production Structure*, Belknap Press of Harvard University Press

LAL, D. (1975), *Appraising Foreign Investment in Developing Countries*, Heinemann

LAMB, H. H. (1966), *The Changing Climate*, Methuen

LAMB, H. H. (1977), *Climate: Present, Past and Future*, vol. 2, *Climatic History and the Future*, Methuen

LANDSBERG, H. E., et al. (1965), *World Map of Climatology*, Springer-Verlag

LANDSBERG, H. H., et al. (1963), *Resources in America's Future: Patterns of Requirements and Availabilities*, Johns Hopkins University Press

LATHAM, A. J. H. (1978), *The International Economy and the Under-developed World 1865–1914*, Croom Helm

LEBERGOTT, S. (1980), 'The returns to US imperialism, 1890–1929', *Journal of Economic History*, vol. 40, pp. 229–52

LEHMANN, D. (ed.) (1974), *Agrarian Reform and Agrarian Reformism: Studies of Peru, Chile, China and India*, Faber

LEONTIEF, W. W., *et al.* (1977), *The Future of the World Economy*, Oxford University Press

LEWIS, W. A. (1955), *The Theory of Economic Growth*, Allen and Unwin

LEWIS, W. A. (1970), *Tropical Development 1880–1913: Studies in Economic Progress*, Allen and Unwin

LEWIS, W. A. (1978a), *Growth and Fluctuations 1870–1913*, Allen and Unwin

LEWIS, W. A. (1978b), *The Evolution of the International Economic Order*, Princeton University Press

LEYS, C. (1975), *Underdevelopment in Kenya: The Political Economy of Neo-Colonialism*, Heinemann

LIST, F. (1885), *The National System of Political Economy*, Longman, Green and Co. (first published in German 1841)

LOWER, A. R. M. (1973), *Great Britain's Woodyard: British America and the Timber Trade, 1763–1867*, McGill–Queen's University Press

MABOGUNJE, A. L. (1980a), 'The dynamics of centre–periphery relations: the need for a new geography of resource development', *Transactions*, Institute of British Geographers, New Series, vol. 5, pp. 277–96

MABOGUNJE, A. L. (1980b), *The Development Process: A Spatial Perspective*, Hutchinson

MAHFUZUR RAHMAN, A. H. M. (1973), *Export of Manufactures from Developing Countries*, Rotterdam University Press

MAHLER, V. A. (1980), *Dependency Approaches to International Poliitical Economy: A Cross-national Study*, Columbia University Press

MALTHUS, T. R. (1820), *Principles of Political Economy Considered with a View to their Practical Application*; vol. 2 of P. Straffa (ed.), *The Works and Correspondence of David Ricardo*, Cambridge University Press 1951

MANLEY, G. (1957), 'Climatic fluctuations and fuel requirements', *Scottish Geographical Magazine*, vol. 73, pp. 19–28

MANNERS, G. (1971), *The Changing World Market for Iron Ore 1950–1980*, Johns Hopkins University Press

MANNERS, G. (1981), 'Our planet's resources', *Geographical Journal*, vol. 147, pp. 1–22

MARKHAM, S. F. (1942), *Climate and the Energy of Nations*, Oxford University Press

MARSHALL, A. (1890), *Principles of Economics*; 1949 edn, Macmillan

MARSTRAND. P. K. and RUSH, H. (1978), 'Food and agriculture: when enough is not enough – the world food paradox', in C. Freeman and M. Jahoda (eds.), pp. 79–112

MARTIN, G. J. (1973), *Ellsworth Huntington: His Life and Thought*, Archon Books

MAUNDER, W. J. (1970), *The Value of the Weather*, Methuen

MCALLISTER, A. L. (1976), 'Price, technology, and ore reserves', in G. J. S. Govett and M. H. Govett (eds.), *World Mineral Supplies: Assessment and Perspective*, Elsevier, pp. 37–97

MEADOWS, D. H., *et al.* (1972), *The Limits to Growth*, Potomac Associates

MEIER, G. M. and BALDWIN, R. E. (1957), *Economic Development: Theory, History, Policy*, Wiley

MIKESELL, R. F., *et al.* (1971), *Foreign Investment in the Petroleum and Mineral Industries: Case Studies of Investor–Host Country Relations*, Johns Hopkins University Press

MILL, J. S. (1848), *Principles of Political Economy*; 1969 edn, ed. W. Ashley, A. M. Kelley

MITCHELL, B. R. and DEANE, P. (1971), *Abstract of British Historical Statistics*, Cambridge University Press

MORGENSTERN, O. (1963), *On the Accuracy of Economic Observations*, 2nd edn, Princeton University Press

MORTON, K. and TULLOCH, P. (1977), *Trade and Developing Countries*, Croom Helm

MYINT, H. (1964), *The Economics of the Developing Countries*, Hutchinson

NABSETH, L. and RAY, G. F. (eds.) (1974), *The Diffusion of New Industrial Processes: An International Study*, Cambridge University Press

NORTH, D. C. (1955), 'Location theory and regional economic growth', *Journal of Political Economy*, vol. 63, pp. 243–58

NURKSE, R. (1962), *Patterns of Trade and Development*, Blackwell

ONYEMELUKWE, C. C. (1974), *Economic Underdevelopment: An Inside View*, Longman

Organisation for Economic Cooperation and Development (1979) *Interfutures: Facing the Future*, OECD

Parliament of the Commonwealth of Australia (1976), *Policies for Development of Manufacturing Industry*, vol. 1, Commonwealth Printing Office

PARRA, F. R. (1980), 'OPEC oil: recent developments and problems of supplies', in R. Mabro (ed.), *World Energy Issues and Policies*, Oxford University Press, pp. 3–11

PARRY, M. L. (1978), *Climatic Change, Agriculture and Settlement*, Dawson

PEARSE, A. (1980), *Seeds of Plenty, Seeds of Want*, Clarendon Press

PEET, R. (1969), 'The spatial expansion of commercial agriculture in the nineteenth century: a von Thünen interpretation', *Economic Geography*, vol. 45, pp. 283–301

PEET, R. (1972), 'Influences of the British market on agriculture and related economic development in Europe before 1860', *Transactions*, Institute of British Geographers, vol. 56, pp. 1–20

PERLOFF, H. S., *et al.* (1960), *Regions, Resources and Economic Growth*, University of Nebraska Press

PERLOFF, H. S. and DODDS, V. W. (1963), *How a Region Grows: Area Development in the US Economy*, Committee for Economic Development

PERLOFF, H. S. and WINGO, L. (1964), 'Natural resource endowment and regional economic growth', in J. Friedmann and W. Alonso (eds.), *Regional Development and Planning: A Reader*, MIT Press, pp. 215–39; first published in J. J. Spengler (ed.) (1961) *Natural Resources and Economic Growth*, Resources for the Future Inc., pp. 191–212

PETTERSSON, O. (1914), *Climatic Variations in Historic and Prehistoric Time*, Springer (first published in Swedish 1913)

President's Materials Policy Commission (1952), *Resources for Freedom*, US Government Printing Office

PRESTWICH, R. (1975), 'America's dependence on the world's metal resources: shifts in import emphasis', *Transactions*, Institute of British Geographers, vol. 64, pp. 97–118

REDDAWAY, W. B., *et al.* (1968), *Effects of UK Direct Investment Overseas: Final Report*, Cambridge University Press

RICARDO, D. (1817), *The Principles of Political Economy and Taxation*; in P. Straffa (ed.), *The Works and Correspondence of David Ricardo*, Cambridge University Press 1951

ROBINSON, E. A. G. (1931), *The Structure of Competitive Industry*, Cambridge University Press

ROBINSON, E. A. G. (ed.) (1960), *Economic Consequences of the Size of Nations*, Macmillan

ROBINSON, E. A. G. (ed.) (1979), *Appropriate Technologies for Third World Development*, Macmillan

ROSTOW, W. W. (1953), *The Process of Economic Growth*, Clarendon Press

ROSTOW, W. W. (1960), *The Stages of Economic Growth: A Non-Communist Manifesto*, Cambridge University Press

ROSTOW, W. W. (1978), *The World Economy: History and Prospect*, Macmillan

ROUTH, G. (1975), *The Origins of Economic Ideas*, Macmillan

LE ROY LADURIE, E. (1972), 'History and climate' (first published in French 1959), in P. Burke (ed.), *Economy and Society in Early Modern Europe*, Routledge and Kegan Paul, pp. 134–69

Royal Institute of International Affairs (1937), *The Colonial Problem*, Oxford University Press

RUSSEL, R. J. (1956), 'Environmental changes through forces independent of man', in W. L. Thomas, *et al*. (eds.), *Man's Role in Changing the Face of the Earth*, University of Chicago Press, pp. 453–70

SAHA, K. R. and MOOLEY, D. A. (1978), 'Fluctuation of monsoon rainfall and crop production', in K. Takahashi and M. M. Yoshino (eds.) pp. 73–80

DOS SANTOS, T. (1970), 'The structure of dependence', *American Economic Review: Papers and Proceedings*, vol. 60, pp. 231–6

SAUER, C. O. (1956), 'The agency of man on the earth', in W. L. Thomas, *et al*. (eds.), *Man's Role in Changing the Face of the Earth*, University of Chicago Press, pp. 49–69

SAUL, S. B. (1960), *Studies in British Overseas Trade 1870–1914*, Liverpool University Press

SCHLEBECKER, J. T. (1960), 'The world metropolis and the history of American agriculture', *Journal of Economic History*, vol. 20, pp. 147–208

SCHUMPETER, J. A. (1949), *The Theory of Economic Development*, Harvard University Press, (first published in German 1911)

SCHUMPETER, J. A. (1954), *History of Economic Analysis*, Allen and Unwin

SEERS, D. (1970) 'The stages of economic growth of a primary producer in the middle of the twentieth century', in R. I. Rhodes (ed.), *Imperialism and Underdevelopment: A Reader*, Monthly Review Press, pp. 163–80

SEERS, D., *et al*. (eds.) (1979), *Underdeveloped Europe: Studies in Core–Periphery Relations*, Harvester Press

SEMPLE, E. C. (1911), *Influences of Geographic Environment*, Constable

SEN, A. K. (1960), *Choice of Techniques: An Aspect of the Theory of Planned Economic Development*, Blackwell

SIMPSON, G. C. (1926), 'Climatic changes', in E. Huntington, *The Pulse of Progress: Including a Sketch of Jewish History*, Scribner, pp. 109–20

SINGER, C., *et al*. (eds.) (1954), *A History of Technology*, vol. 1, Oxford University Press

SINGER, C., *et al*. (eds.) (1956), *A History of Technology*, vol. 2, Oxford University Press

SINGER, H. W. and ANSARI, J. A. (1977), *Rich and Poor Countries*, Allen and Unwin

SLICHER VAN BATH, B. H. (1963), *The Agrarian History of Western Europe AD 500–1850*, Arnold, (first published in Dutch)

SMITH, A. (1776), *An Inquiry into the Nature and Causes of the Wealth of Nations*; annotated version of 5th edn, ed. E. Cannan, Methuen 1950

STRAHLER, A. N. (1969), *Physical Geography*, 3rd edn, Wiley

SUPPLE, B. E. (1963), 'Economic history, economic theory, and economic growth', in B. E. Supple (ed.) *The Experience of Economic Growth: Case Studies in Economic History*, Random House, pp. 1–46

SUPPLE, B. E. (1972), 'Thinking about economic development', in A. J.

Youngson (ed.), *Economic Development in the Long Run*, Allen and Unwin, pp. 19–35

TAKAHASHI, K. and NEMOTO, J. (1978), 'Relationship between climatic change, rice production, and population', in K. Takahashi and M. M. Yoshino (eds.), pp. 183–96

TAKAHASHI, K. and YOSHINO, M. M. (eds.) (1978), *Climatic Change and Food Production*, University of Tokyo Press

TAWNEY, R. H. (1926), *Religion and the Rise of Capitalism: A Historical Study*, Murray

THIRLWALL, A. P. (1978), *Growth and Development: With Special Reference to Developing Economies*, Macmillan

THORNTHWAITE, C. W. (1948), 'An approach toward a rational classification of climate', *Geographical Review*, vol. 38, pp. 55–94

TOYNBEE, A. J. (1934–59), *A Study of History*, 11 vols. Oxford University Press

TREWARTHA, G. T. (1954), *An Introduction to Climate*, McGraw-Hill

TREWARTHA, G. T. (1961), *The Earth's Problem Climates*, University of Wisconsin Press

UCHIJIMA, Z. (1978), 'Long-term change and variability of air temperature above 10°C in relation to crop production', in K. Takahashi and M. M. Yoshino (eds.), pp. 217–29

UNESCO (1979), *Map of the World Distribution of Arid Regions*, MAB Technical Notes 7

United Nations (1980), *Human Settlements in the Arctic*, Pergamon

UTTERSTRÖM, G. (1955), 'Climatic fluctuations and population problems in early modern history', *Scandinavian Economic History Review*, vol. 3, pp. 3–47

VAN VALKENBURG, S. and HELD, C. (1952), *Europe*, 2nd edn, Wiley

VANEK, J. (1959), 'The natural resource content of foreign trade, 1870–1955, and the relative abundance of natural resources in the United States', *Review of Economics and Statistics*, vol. 41, pp. 146–53

DE VRIES, J. (1974), *The Dutch Rural Economy in the Golden Age, 1500–1700*, Yale University Press

WAGLE, D. M. (1981), 'Imperial preference and the Indian steel industry, 1924–39', *Economic History Review*, vol. 34, pp. 120–31

WALLERSTEIN, I. (1974), *The Modern World System: Capitalistic Agriculture and the Origins of the European World-economy in the Sixteenth Century*, Academic Press

WAN, H. Y. (1971), *Economic Growth*, Harcourt Brace Jovanovich

WARRINER, D. (1939), *Economics of Peasant Farming*, Oxford University Press

WARRINER, D. (1969), *Land Reform in Principle and Practice*, Clarendon Press

WATKINS, M. H. (1963), 'A staple theory of economic growth', *Canadian Journal of Economics and Political Science*, vol. 29, pp. 141–58

WEBER, M. (1976), *The Protestant Ethic and the Spirit of Capitalism*, Allen and Unwin (first published in German 1904–5; English trans. first published 1930)

WEBER, A. (1929), *Theory of the Location of Industries*, University of Chicago Press (first published in German 1909)

WHITTLESEY, D. (1949), *Environmental Foundations of European History*, Appleton-Century-Crofts

WOLFF, R. D. (1974), *The Economics of Colonialism: Britain and Kenya, 1870–1930*, Yale University Press

World Bank (1976), *World Bank Atlas: Population*, per capita *Product and Growth Rates*, World Bank

World Bank (1981), *1980 World Bank Atlas: Population,* per capita *Product, and Growth Rates*, World Bank

World Energy Conference (1980), *Survey of Energy Resources 1980*, World Energy Conference

WRIGHT, H. E. (1977), 'Environmental change and the origin of agriculture in the Old and New Worlds', in C. A. Reed (ed.), *Origins of Agriculture*, Mouton, pp. 281–318

WRIGLEY, E. A. (1962a), 'The supply of materials in the Industrial Revolution', *Economic History Review*, vol. 15, pp. 1–16

WRIGLEY, E. A. (1962b), *Industrial Growth and Population Change: A Regional Study of the Coalfield Areas of North-West Europe in the Later Nineteenth Century*, Cambridge University Press

YOUNG, A. A. (1928), 'Increasing returns and economic progress', *Economic Journal*, vol. 38, pp. 527–42

YOUNGSON, A. J. (1959), *Possibilities of Economic Progress*, Cambridge University Press

YOUNGSON, A. J. (1967), *Overhead Capital: A Study in Development Economics*, Edinburgh University Press

Index

Uchijima, Z., 182
underdevelopment, 76–81
unequal exchange, 51–2, 70–1
Utterström, G., 164, 173

Van Valkenburg, S., 174
Vanek, J., 36
villagization, 151, 152
De Vries, J., 48

wages, 102, 103, 108, 138, 139
Wagle, D.M., 89
Wallerstein, I., 187, 188
Wan, H.Y., 37, 43
Warriner, D., 85, 150
Watkins, M.H., 120
wealth: definition of, 14
Weber, A., 120
Weber, M., 159, 160, 161
Whittlesey, D., 166
Wingo, L., 126
Wolff, R.D., 69
Wright, H.E., 176
Wrigley, E.A., 112, 122, 124

Yamey, B.S., 37
Yoshino, M.M., 180
Young, A.A., 53
Youngson, A.J., 53, 55, 56, 87, 111

Zötl, J.G., 176